JOURNEY TO THE *Aisle*

...a Story of Cultural Expectations

CARMEN TREVIÑO MORENO

Library of Congress Control Number: 2024943875
                         Paperback: 979-8-89306-073-7
                         eBook: 979-8-89306-074-4

Printed in the United States of America

Contents

Dedication

To Juan, the man in my life, who has taught me more than I could have ever imagined about love, and life. His life in the Raymondville barrio surrounded by Mexican music and Tex-Mex Spanish has continued to be a personal learning experience for me. To date I have a difficult time understanding some of his vocabulary but have learned a completely new sublanguage known as Tex-Mex. I have also learned to appreciate the incredibly reflective words used in so many of the Mexican ranchera songs he continues to enjoy listening to this day.

Life is full of challenges. For me, deciding to walk down the wedding aisle required a cup overflowing with reflection, commitment, tenacity, and a belief that picking whom you want to spend the rest of your life with does not require a prescription as dictated by a parent. However, life brings greater challenges as years come and go. The commonalities that drew us to each other have been a great source of strength. However, our differences are what have created the greatest of all challenges in this journey of life and learning.

To my dear children Carmen Cecilia, Juan Jaime, Tomas Daniel, and Roberto Antonio, who have also taught me so much about the privilege of being their mother and the challenges of being their parent—the most difficult job I ever had in my life. My love for each of you only grows deeper as I continue to watch you grow, mature, and be successful with your lives. I am so proud of all of you. In addition, of course, Cecilia, thank you for bringing into the world Bryan and Ryan. Being a grandmother has been the easiest job of my life, and I have loved every minute of it.

Carmen Treviño Moreno

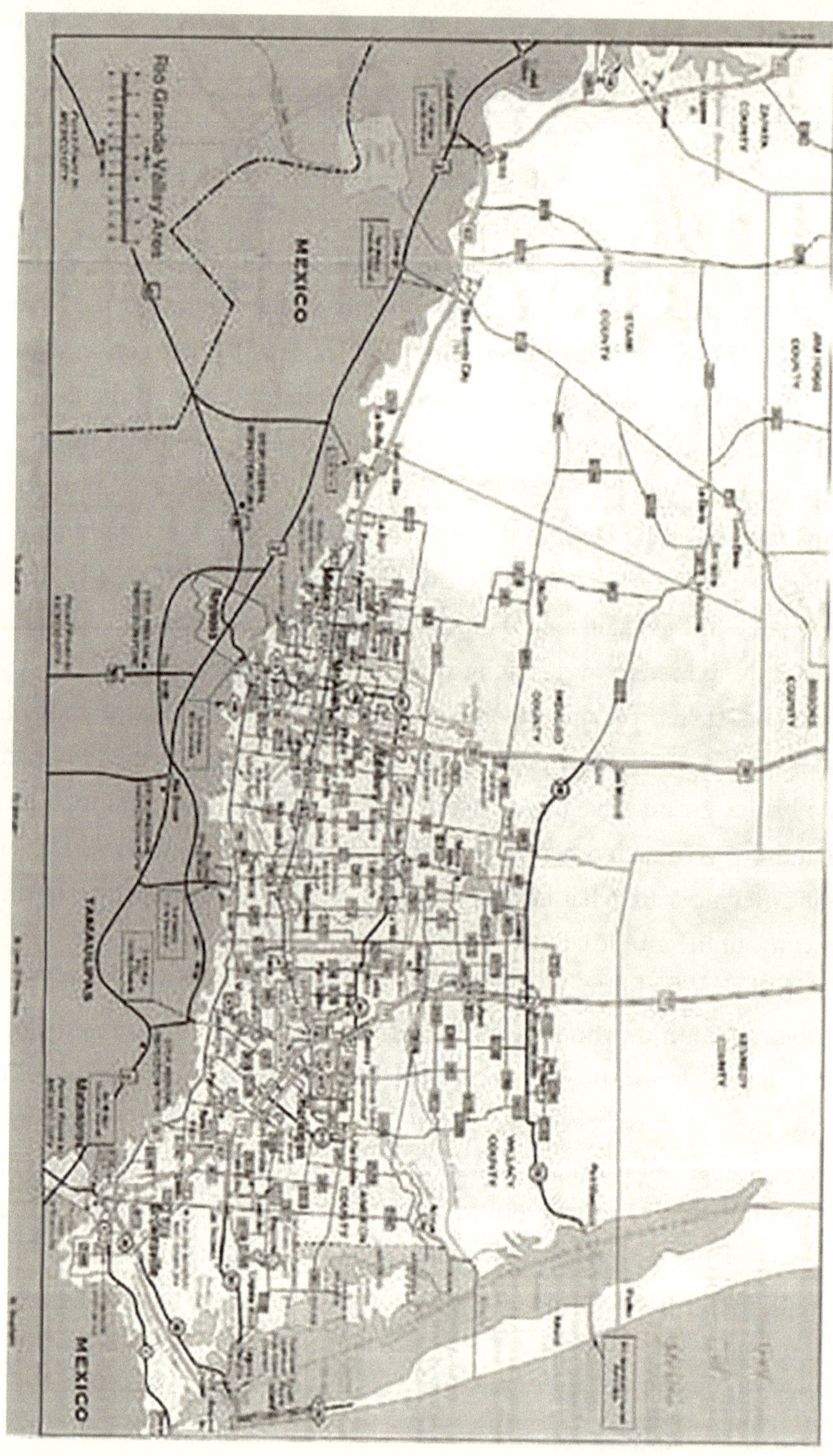

Rio Grande Valley Area
MEXICO
MEXICO
TAMAULIPAS
TAMAULIPAS
STARR COUNTY
HIDALGO COUNTY
WILLACY COUNTY
CAMERON COUNTY

Foreword

Cities destroy customs, very simply stated in a Mexican ranchera song "Las Ciudades" by Jose Alfredo Jimenez, conveys a depth of truth unrealized. We have evolved into families separated by hundreds and thousands of miles geographically because of marriages and chosen careers. This evolution has also created a diminishing and even an elimination of so many cultural traditions that were the norm and center of social interactions half a century ago in many of our families. European traditions, brought to the United States by our ancestors via Mexico, have disappeared with the second and third generation born in America. The daily diet of homemade flour and corn tortillas, carne guisada, picadillo, arroz con pollo, frijolitos, caldo, papas con huevo, chorizo con huevos, tamales, empanadas, pan de polvo, and buñuelos have all but disappeared from the art of home cooking to the fast-food world longing to satisfy our innate cultural taste buds.

Having been born the second child in a family of eleven children (eight sisters and three brothers), at a very young age I learned responsibility by helping Mamá with many household chores and spending a lot of time in the kitchen. By the time I was twelve years old, I could cook a full meal for the entire family, making homemade flour tortillas, corn tortillas using the tortillera, guisados and sopas, and baking all sorts of yeast breads, cakes, pies, and cookies. I thought nothing of it. I believed all families reared their children the same way. I knew what the expectations were, and the unwritten rule was to meet those expectations without any excuses. The thought of questioning those expectations never entered my mind. To win my parents' approval, I was expected to go to school, make good grades, come home, do my homework, help with the cooking, clean the kitchen daily, and help the younger siblings with their homework.

In relating this story to you, my children, I hope you do not conclude that there are too many insignificant details addressed. The details are essential in relating the many true stories of how historical events, cultural influences, Catholic teachings, expectations, norms, and human experiences that come with living a life rich with traditional customs become the core of our being, forever influencing decisions throughout our lives. Not one of us can change our origin of birth. I have yet to meet anyone who has changed the environment they were born into; however, I have met many people who have chosen to improve their future by moving away from their roots, studying, and working hard in hopes of improving the conditions that surrounded them at birth. The intent of this writing is to share with you true-life stories and experiences from my growing-up years. The following is what I remember seeing, hearing, feeling, thinking, learning, experiencing, and living as I grew up in the barrio in Pharr, Texas, on the west side of town, on the other side of the tracks.

This endeavor is merely an attempt to share with you a life experience in the barrio that none of you ever experienced. A life that possibly none of you could ever relate to is, nonetheless, the foundation of a journey that led me to becoming your mother. Surrounded by poverty and lack of education was never an acceptable excuse for not setting goals for a better life, even though I believe I have always had a good life. I am forever grateful to Mamà and Papà for doing the best they knew how to teach me to set goals and for creating a world within our home that set expectations ignoring all outside barriers. I will never forget the *Green, Green Grass of Home*, or my roots!

Mil Gracias

Thank you to my siblings, Lee, Teresa, Luis, Margaret, Henry, and Rosie for your endless patience as you listened to my reflections and answered my endless inquiries that validated many of my memories. As always, *mucho cariño y abrazos* to all.

West Hawk Street

Give me a land of boughs in leaf, A land of trees that stand. Where trees are fallen, there is grief; I love no leafless land.
- Alfred Edward Housman

I grew up surrounded by stability. Hispanic families living in the barrio during the 40s and 50s were supposedly poor and uneducated, but steadfast in the practice of family values and traditions.

I lived in the same home on the 200 block of West Hawk Street just a block west of the Old Military Highway 281 going south in Pharr, Texas, until my wedding day. All the wood-frame homes resonated with people completely oblivious to the existence of a larger world breathing outside this geographical area. They exhibited their small multicolored flower gardens every spring with great pride and dignity. The flowers cared for meticulously were destined for our Blessed Virgin Mary to enjoy as an offering during her month of May. Every inch of land produced an array of color for our eyes to enjoy or nourishment for our bodies. Our home sitting in a piece of land only 50 feet wide and 140 feet long was surrounded on each side by fruit-bearing trees: an avocado tree, several papaya trees, a huge pecan tree on Papa Grande's property next door, a fig tree, a guava tree, a lemon tree, and an orange tree. The front of our home manicured with carpet grass on each side looked like spring year round. Along each side of the sidewalk leading to the steps of the entrance to the house, I was greeted year-round with pink and red zinnias; yellow and orange marigolds; deep red geraniums; and white, pink, and purple periwinkles. Mamá labored year-round to keep her flowers blooming. The smell of gardenias and roses alongside the dividing fence between my grandparents' home and ours reached my nostrils as soon as I walked on the sidewalk past Papa Grande's home. The scent of the gardenias came through our bedroom windows as the Rio Grande Valley breeze blew from the south to cool our non-air-conditioned home.

Families who lived on our block worked very hard and survived by using the skills they had to make a living. At the front of the lot, directly across the street from our home, a family owned a *sastrería* (tailor's shop). Behind the one-room, family-operated business was their home. At the end of the block lived an older woman in the very back of the lot in a two-room home, Doña Pepa, who made a living as a seamstress. Across the street from her, on our side of the street next to my grandparents' home, was Don Panchito with his *tiendita* (small store). Don Panchito was an elderly man whose *tiendita* was also located in front of his home. A screen door at the very edge of the sidewalk accessed the small storefront property with one refrigerator displaying soda, milk, and eggs; one checkout counter; shelves on the wall for a few canned items; and a large display of an assortment of penny candy in opened glass jars. The thick glass jars displaying candy cigarettes, bubble gum cigars, wax Coke-shaped bottles with colored sugar water inside, Bazooka bubble gum, Kits in different flavors (banana, strawberry, chocolate), tricolored coconut flags, bright-colored gumballs, all flavors of lollipops, candy buttons on paper, candy bracelets, and Sugar Daddy caramel suckers took more than half of the store at the very entrance. The barrio children anxiously waited for the candy wholesale delivery truck owned by Don Mauro Perez from Mission to drive down the street. New candy had arrived at Don Panchito's tiendita! That was our signal! We walked fast with pennies and nickels in hand to take care of our sugar cravings. By midafternoon, Don Panchito would be frustrated with all of us "niños necios que vienen con un mugroso centavo cada rato" (bothersome children that come over to spend just a dirty penny every minute).

On the opposite corner of the block on the same side as our home lived the Tijerinas in an unpainted two-story home. The grandmother,

mother, and daughter who resided in that home also had a business selling remedies, teas, and candles. The all-female family was eccentric, and it was common knowledge in the barrio that they were *brujas* and practiced *brujerías*. *Brujería* is the Spanish word for witchcraft and refers to a mystical sect that practices rituals using herbs and candles. I recall visiting that house only once. Mamá needed some manzanilla (chamomile) tea leafs to make tea for one of my sisters who had the stomach flu. The front door led me to a huge room—very dark, dreary, and musty smelling—full of shelves filled with bags full of tea leafs. Candles were also displayed everywhere. It was a very scary, eerie-feeling place. I never went back! Across the street from them lived a man who fixed lawnmowers for a living. People struggled to feed their families, but it is now obvious to me that there was no lack of entrepreneurship in the barrio.

Just around the corner on Aster Street was a larger grocery store with a meat market that the Villarreals owned. Across from them was my favorite "La Reynera Panadería" (bakery). About three o'clock in the afternoon throughout the barrio we could smell the aroma of the baking of *pan dulce: empanadas* and *molletes*. It was a reminder to get ready for the midafternoon *merienda*, the traditional time in Mexico to take a break and have some sweet bread with coffee. During the very hot summer months, instead of drinking coffee with our pan dulce, we would indulge in a Kool-Aid drink. All the icons of the influence of a barrio rich in a Mexican lifestyle resonated with the sounds of the Spanish language, the aroma of tortillas cooking on the grill, and from the alley behind our home the radio blaring the sounds of the música norteña. Just a block from my favorite bakery going south was the railroad track that runs parallel to Business Highway 83 known as Center Street. Every time I needed to go to the downtown area to the drugstore or Hanshaw's 5¢&10¢, I had to walk through this area. I was always a nervous wreck when I walked in front of the cantina, the barbershop, and the billiards place located across the street from the bakery. I was terrified of the men who would just be *Standing on the Corner*, leaning against the walls, staring at you while making all kinds of comments, whistling, and making gestures as I walked by. I realize it was an expected behavior for men in the barrio to react that way when a young girl walked by. However, I dreaded that experience every time. We were only eleven miles from Mexico's border! Of course, these behaviors were acceptable in our culture.

Within a six-block area, one could find any type of business you needed to frequent—from *tienditas, panaderías, sastrería, tortillerías,* mercantile, *mueblería, barbería,* garages, to cantinas (small grocery stores, bakeries, dry cleaners, tortilla factory, miscellaneous-goods store, furniture store, barbershop, garages, and bars).

The Catholic church, St. Margaret Mary, was just at the corner of the 100 block on West Hawk Street, less than a block from our home. Everyone in the barrio walked to Mass on Sunday morning and to all the devotionals held throughout the year: October, the month to recite the Rosary daily in the evening; the missions held in Spanish during lent; and the recitation of the Rosary and offering of fresh flowers to our Blessed Mother Mary during the month of May. Life surrounded us with families rich in hope and a sense of endurance and perseverance, accepting whatever life brought with a depth of faith measurable only by the Supreme Being.

St. Margaret Mary Catholic Church, Pharr, TX

The Irish Nuns

'Tis education forms the common mind; just as the twig is bent the tree's inclined.

- Alexander Pope, An Essay on Man

Attending St. Margaret's Catholic School for the first eight years of my education was a unique experience evolving into a very beneficial futuristic asset unbeknownst to me at the time. Why? Living in the Mexican barrio in Pharr, Texas, where the majority of parents did not speak English, was not exactly an environment where you would expect to get an Irish Catholic education in the 50s. My brothers, sisters, and I attended elementary school daily with Irish nuns, Sisters of the Holy Ghost, who came to the United States at the end of every summer directly from Ireland to teach us during the school year. Papá was part of a group of community leaders who decided that they did not want their children to go to public schools, so they started working with Bishop M. S. Garriga of the Corpus Christi Catholic Diocese to plan for the building of a Catholic school. The school opened before my sixth birthday in September in 1950; and many of us, along with many of the neighborhood kids, went to St. Margaret's Catholic School through the eighth grade. What a great vision Papá had to provide a quality education to a group of Hispanics *en el barrio*! What an immeasurable impact this initiative had in preparing a hardworking, poverty-stricken community for an enhanced quality of life that future generations would reap. This experience has been one of the greatest assets my parents gave me.

Classes were small, everyone knew everybody, and the nuns spoke only English. The school was a two-story brick building with tall crank-opening windows. It was the only brick building, other than the church, in the barrio. The mother superior, Sister Mary Genevieve, was the only non-Irish nun; she was from Germany. The first week she arrived, she went to Papá and asked him to teach her all the Spanish curse words so she could understand what the students were saying and punish the ones who cursed. I sincerely believe Papá did because she always managed to catch the boys that used foul language. One time in the fourth grade, she heard Edward saying bad words. She stopped class, gave us a writing assignment, and went to the convent, located on the same grounds adjacent to the school. She was gone for just a few minutes. We did not dare move an inch, wondering what she was going to do. We knew it was not going to be pleasant. We sat at our desks like statues, moving only our writing hand as Mother Superior instructed. She came back within ten minutes and had a bar of soap in her hand. She returned. "Edward, go to the front of the class and stand there. Stick out your tongue," she commanded. She took the bar of soap and rubbed his tongue with it several times. He gagged horribly while giving her the most evil look I have ever seen. Gasping for relief, his body shivering, he ran to the water fountain to cleanse his taste buds of that experience.

We were terrified of Sister Genevieve's presence. She was a very matronly looking woman who never smiled. "Fear me" was the invisible message written all over her face. Edward was always a problem student, and before he finished his eighth year in school, he served time in the county jail. I recall in the seventh grade when our class would pray the Rosary daily in hopes that Edward would learn to stay out of trouble and return to school. He remained in jail a lot of the time but managed to finish the eighth-grade year.

It was common knowledge of Papa's involvement with the building of the school, so the nuns had great respect for him. It was also difficult for us at times to be from the Loreto Treviño family. Since I started taking piano lessons in the second grade, by the time I was in the fourth grade, I had already learned how to play the only organ the church owned. It was a pump organ, a very demanding instrument because the player had to maintain the air pressure needed for creating the sound in the free reeds by pumping the two pedals with both feet. It was hard work! I would get leg cramps in the middle of the night after a long practice.

Sister Mary Grace, a tall, slim, and stern-faced nun who never smiled, tutored me through the learning process. I recall during a very long practice after school, in the sixth grade, I had a difficult time with the playing of the Gloria as we were preparing for Holy Week. Sister kept asking me to play a few bars of the music and insisted I was playing one wrong note. I looked and looked over the music, and I could not figure out what I was doing wrong. I just kept playing it as she ordered it. My frustration became evident by the fifth time I played the same bars repeatedly. Sister yelled at me with, "Just because you're Loreto Treviño's daughter does not mean you can do what you want. Do as I say and play it right." I was emotionally devastated hearing those words. "Because I was Loreto Treviño's daughter"! What did that have to do with this? What did that mean? Was it a bad thing to be my father's daughter? I started sobbing like a baby. The tears kept coming uncontrollably. I could not stop. She sent everyone home within a few minutes, and I ran to my classroom across the hall to pick up my books to take home for homework. She followed me and tried to talk to me, asking me to calm down because she had not done anything wrong. I just could not stop crying, could not say a word, never looked at her face, and left the classroom as fast as I could to walk home. I walked very slowly through the alley that led directly to our home about half a block away. All I could think about was why she was so insulting and mean. She embarrassed me in front of all my classmates. How could I face them tomorrow? I did not understand what she meant by her statement, but it hurt! I certainly did not pick my parents. I still have not met anyone who has!

By the time I got home, I was calmer; but, of course, Mamá knew something was wrong just by looking at my flushed face. I explained what happened, and as I was trying to relate the happening, the phone rings. It was Sister Grace. She wanted my mother to know that she did not understand why I became so upset during the practice. She wanted Mamá to understand that she had done nothing to cause my emotional outburst. Mamá stayed calm as usual, and she told me that Sister was probably in a bad mood and had run out of patience. Mama's patience and tolerance were immeasurable! Everyone knew of Sister Grace's bad moods and the fact that she never smiled. We left it at that. No one ever brought up that incident again, but I never forgot how hurtful words could be. This incident merely reinforced my introvert personality. I learned to continue sitting at my desk, do as I am told, watch my surroundings, listen, answer a question only if asked, and think, think, think!

I had many other nuns as teachers whose personalities were very different. Sister Benignus (my eighth-grade teacher) and Sister Mary William (my sixth-grade teacher) were very calm and gentle in their approach, and I do not recall ever hearing them raise their voice or show anger. Their wearing of the habit was enough to demand our respect. Respecting all religious, and elders, regardless of who they were, was reinforced at home daily. The nuns emphasized reading, writing, penmanship, English grammar, spelling, vocabulary, and mathematics. Of course, the Baltimore Catechism and Bible study with daily homework were part of the daily assignments. Each nun taught at least two grades; if a grade level reached more than twenty students, then one nun would teach only that grade. They dedicated their lives to teaching. They were always prepared for class, and I do not remember ever having a day off from reading, writing, and learning.

I do not recall ever learning anything about Mexican music, Cinco de Mayo, Dieciseis de Septiembre, the Ballet Folklórico, or anything Spanish or Mexican. However, we learned how to dance the Irish jig and celebrate St. Patrick's Day and St. Joseph's Day with an annual program presented on March 17. To honor St. Patrick annually, we all dressed in Kelly green full skirts and golden blouses with Kelly green vests made of taffeta material. We learned to sing "When Irish Eyes Are Smiling," "Danny Boy," and always finished the school program with the hymn "Hail, Glorious St. Patrick." I recall one program when I played the piano, accompanying a fiddle player playing the Irish jig.

In addition, we learned American history, lined up daily to say the Pledge of Allegiance prior to going into the classrooms, and sang the national anthem and "America the Beautiful." Daily, we recited the prayer to our guardian angel, the Morning Offering to the Sacred Heart, the Lord's Prayer, the Hail Mary, and the Glory as soon as we entered the classroom; the Angelus before lunch break; and a Prayer of Thanksgiving after lunch. Some days before leaving for home in the afternoon, we recited the Rosary. Recess was also part of the day, but not everyday. We did not attend daily Mass, but we did attend Mass every first Friday. Church missals were printed in Latin on one side and English on the other. For weekend masses, the missals were printed in Latin on one side and Spanish on the other. I challenged myself by studying the words in Latin and learning the translations in either English or Spanish. The school day was structured daily, rarely deviating from the scheduled activities.

As an adult, I am still amazed at how we all survived. The nuns did the best they could do, including exposing us to the art of singing and dancing even though it was all Irish songs and dances and, of course, all of the church music that we learned to read in Latin. Papá told me I had to learn to play the piano for the specific purpose of later learning how to play the church organ and prepare to learn the hymns and different masses for the liturgical year. How could we expect the nuns to teach us anything from our own culture? They came directly from their mother country not ever having any prior knowledge of any other culture. Many of them were in their early twenties. That was all they knew! They spoke only English; the great majority of us spoke only Spanish. No one had a clue what bilingual education was! We were one of the fortunate families who had both parents that spoke both English and Spanish. We also had an advantage in that Mamá had been a primary-school teacher prior to marrying Papá, and she prepared us for the first year of school, teaching us the typical curriculum taught in kindergarten. I entered school knowing the alphabet, numbers, and letter sounds in English. I also knew what a blackboard and chalk were because Mamá used to have us play school at home. We had books at home that Mom read to us in both English and Spanish.

The nuns ran the school and the convent without any outside hired help. The parish consisted of hardworking, poor families. The parents volunteered to help with any work needed like painting, lawn work, cleaning, and cooking for the annual picnic for the students. The nuns dedicated themselves to their work in educating us and never socialized outside of their order. About twice a year, they walked to our home, a half block from the corner of the church, for a special dinner Mamá prepared them. Seeing the nuns walking through the neighborhood in their striking black habits was a stunning sight for the families in the barrio always looking out the windows. Mamá always served the same menu. Iceberg lettuce leafs with a pineapple ring and cherry salad in the middle, baked chicken made with a tomato-and-mustard sauce, rice, green vegetables, hot biscuits, and a homemade lemon meringue pie for dessert. They seamed to enjoy the only break they got from their kitchen duties. It was forbidden for us children to be in the living room or dining room when adults were invited over as guests. We had to stay in our bedrooms until they left.

By the time I was in the sixth grade at the age of twelve, three of us students—Susie, Ella, and I—helped the nuns with cleaning the convent hardwood floors, the school bathrooms, and the windows. Since we had hardwood floors at home, I knew the process of cleaning, waxing, and buffing the hardwood floors. I would help Mamá with those chores at home regularly. About every two weeks, we left the classroom early on Fridays and go to the convent to clean. On our knees, we would scrub the floors, apply the wax by hand, and then use the electric buffer to shine the floors. We always started with the downstairs floor and then continued with the chapel that was located on the second floor. It usually took us four to five hours to finish cleaning. We never cleaned the nuns' bedrooms. We were forbidden to enter their bedrooms.

Mamá and Papá never complained about any assignments we got from the nuns even though Papá always told us that none of his daughters were to ever work anywhere as maids or waitresses. They accepted that assignment as part of the need to keep the school alive and running. Our reward from the nuns was usually a cold drink with a sandwich from them before we left for home. A sandwich was actually a treat because we only ate sandwiches at home once a week on Saturday evenings so Mamá could get a break from having to cook a hot meal. In addition, the sandwiches consisted of very unusual ingredients like Spam and pineapple jam. I was not used to that type of food. Our sandwiches at home were made with bologna or lunch meat, cheese, lettuce, tomatoes, and pickles. Sweet-tasting sandwiches were foreign to my taste buds, but I enjoyed them.

We, as students, managed to survive daily, moving from the Irish-Catholic-dominant school environment to the, in my case, European-Spanish-Italian customs and expectations that had to be adhered to at home. Adding to the environment was our mental immersion into the white Anglo-Saxon lifestyles as depicted on television shows. We watched TV as a family on weekends and whenever we were done with homework and chores; it was our connection to an unknown world yet to be discovered.

Our exposure to popular music was mostly to American music from watching television and all the popular shows of the 50s. *I Love Lucy, The Honeymooners, Father Knows Best, The Ed Sullivan Show, The Lawrence Welk Show, Your Hit Parade,* and *The Dick Clark Show* were all regulars in our household. Many evenings, all the kids from the neighborhood came over to our house, sat on the living floor, and watched TV with us since we were the only household in our block that had a TV for several years. Papa bought our first TV in 1950. We all stared at it for at least five minutes until it warmed up. For some reason we kept looking at the snowy screen, expecting it to change in a second. It never did!

We never missed *The Ed Sullivan Show* on Sunday evenings. The first time Elvis appeared on the show, Papá commented on how that crazy kid could be allowed to be on TV, looking like that with long hair and moving his body like an idiot. Of course, we were glued to the TV, enjoying every minute of the show!

Every piece of clothing we wore was ironed. I even ironed pillowcases, dishtowels, and Papa's underwear. On Saturday mornings as I did all the ironing, I listened to KRIO radio rock station from McAllen and KURV country station from Edinburgh. We learned many of the traditional Western songs from watching Roy Rogers and Gene Autry as they sang along the dusty roads during their TV shows. Papá especially liked the Western shows that always had the *bandidos* dressed in black against the good cowboys always dressed in white; the good guys always won the fights.

Both Mamá and Papá loved music. They always encouraged us to sing and dance in the living-room floor while watching TV. Papá even bought us the piano music sheets for the popular songs sung in *Your Hit Parade* so we could learn how to play them at home on our piano. We would write a list of Papa's favorite songs that he enjoyed listening to on *Your Hit Parade* and give it to our piano teacher for her to buy the sheet music at the music shop. My sister, Imelda and I played duets of some of the popular boogie-woogie songs. For some reason I always got what I thought was the difficult part, the bass clef. Imelda was born with a talent I did not have. She could play anything by just listening to the tune and improvising; I had to learn to read the music before my tapping of the piano keys sounded like a familiar tune. In our geographical area, Spanish television programs were not transmitted, so listening to the TV programs in English enhanced our learning of the language.

The nuns did a great job as teachers. They stressed structure and self-discipline, the study of the three Rs, listening, obedience, manners, and respect at all times. I am convinced that foundation prepared me for college.

By the time I was in the eighth grade, I seriously considered becoming a nun. At the end of the seventh grade, Sister Mary Grace asked me to consider joining the convent to become a nun. I would have to give up having children if I chose that vocation. I loved children and the nurturing that came with caring for children. I suppose since I helped Mamá so much with my younger sisters, changing their diapers, feeding them their bottles, dressing them, bathing them, and even monitoring them if they got sick, I experienced what nurturing was, so I decided that being a nun was not my calling. That year I decided that somewhere in the distant future I would get married and have my own family. First, I had to get a college education.

The new St. Margaret Mary Catholic Church was built and dedicated in 1953. Mamá and Papá were instrumental in the accomplishment of the project. The tamale-making fundraisers were always held in our home because we had a huge four-car green aluminum garage in the back of the house that was almost as wide as the fifty-foot lot. It was a backbreaking tedious project to prepare a minimum of two hundred dozen tamales to sell for $1.25 per dozen. Several long tables were set up to prepare for the assembly line of señoras that worked on the project. Preparing the meat, mixing the masa, spreading the masa on the prepared husks that had to be soaked for hours before using, filling and wrapping the husks already spread with the masa, and finally placing them in the huge pots for simmering until done. This all-day, labor-intensive project started by seven in the morning and ended by seven in the evening if enough señoras showed up to help. It was always a great gathering event for all the señoras from the "barrio" and a time to share all the family stories. I could see Mamá was happy to be involved in this. What an opportunity to interact with other women and break the daily monotony of caring for Papá and us. *Las señoras* and *comadres* caught up with all the events going on in their families. Whose daughter became a "señorita" (a reference used for a young girl who has reached puberty and had started her menstrual period) and who was courting who and, of course, parents worried, wondering who was going to elope with the first boy that fell in love with them. Many young couples in love decided to elope especially if the bride's family did not approve of the groom or the girl got pregnant after sneaking out with the unapproved boyfriend. It was also an opportunity for the comadres to catch up with all the barrio gossip.

St. Margaret Mary School, 1950-1970, Pharr, TX

St. Margaret Convent, back entrance

Los Abuelos

See how many are better off than you are, but consider how many are worse.

- Séneca

Adhering to traditional customs was family law. Papa's parents lived next door to us. When Papa Grande Alejo Treviño (my father's dad) passed away at the age of ninety-one, it became an event that has remained imprinted in my mind. Papa Grande fell in the backyard at the age of eighty-nine and broke a hip. Mama Grande Margarita Martinez Treviño-Treviño, his third wife, was fourteen years younger than he was but unable to care for him on a daily basis. Papa Grande's first wife died giving birth to their first child. His second wife also died giving birth but had already given him two sons who remained in Mexico all their lives. Mama Grande Margarita was his second cousin, and he chose to marry her in order to remain in the same social and economic status, an expected standard in the culture of the Spaniards. She was a matronly looking woman no more than five feet tall who always seemed unhappy. She always sounded bitter and had a stern, very pale-looking face. She hated Pancho Villa for causing the revolution in Mexico.

I remember so many stories that Mama Grande Margarita told us (my sister Imelda, a year older than me, and I) when she was in a storytelling mood and would command us to sit on the floor by her side. Many times, after school, Imelda and I would stop by to greet them, and she would prepare *café con leche* for our enjoyment while she related her stories. The drink was more *leche* than *café*: a small amount of very strong boiled home-brewed coffee and the rest of the cup filled with Carnation milk straight from the can. My addiction to caffeine began as a child. My taste buds were drawn like magnets to the drink. We would just sit there, drink our café con leche, and listen. Sometimes Tía Julia would use the washtub wringer washing machine as we sat listening to Mama Grande's stories. Many times as I sat there staring at the washtub wringer, I wondered if the two rolls on the machine really helped clean the clothes. I did not realize that the rollers were wringing the clothes, not washing them. We never asked a question. We never made a sound. Her tone became harsher and harsher as she told the story about their exodus from Burgos, Mexico—all the land, the hacienda, the three maids, all left behind because of that *condenado mendigó* (condemned beggar) Pancho Villa, as she referred to him time and time again. One housemaid was to take care of the upstairs bedrooms, one was to do the laundry, and another was to help in the kitchen. All daughters were taught the art of being homemakers—cooking; canning fruits and vegetables; embroidery of pillowcases, napkins, doilies, tablecloths; sewing; and quilt making. The family fled for their lives in 1919 or 1920. However, the documentation of border crossings noted that Papa Grande registered Mama Grande, Tía Barbarita, Tía Beatrice, Tía Santos, Tía Carmen, and Tío Julian on September 9, 1928. What happened to the other four—Tío Exiquio the eldest son, Tía Julia the eldest daughter, and the two youngest brothers Papá Loreto and Tío Guadalupe? They were documented as crossing the border a month later on October 2, 1928. Where were they left behind for a month? Tío Exiquio was never documented as crossing the border. Why?

Papá commented on occasion that because all of the Treviño family members were so white skinned, the immigration officers at the U.S. border were reluctant to spray them with a white powder used on all immigrants coming from Mexico to treat them for lice. The officers thought that they looked just like white Americans.

The only items that they brought with them were what fit in the two oxen-driven wagons. One cart carried provisions and personal belongings, and the other carried all of the family members—Papa Grande, Mama Grande, five sons, and five daughters. Mama Grande always talked about the gold pieces that they hid in all of the girls' belts. The girls wore thick wide leather belts around their wastes to keep their very heavy skirts up. The black leather belts had slim pocketlike sections for keeping bullets in case they were needed. In this case, the pockets were filled with gold pieces and gold coins that Papa Grande had saved in his personal safe at the hacienda. That gold was exchanged for money in order to survive when they crossed the border into the United States.

Many times, I wondered why Mama Grande had to reiterate the story repeatedly. I had memorized it by the time I was ten but did not have an appreciation for the details of such a historical event until I became an adult. As I grew older, I wished I had paid more attention to her storytelling. I also came to an understanding as to the reason for her bitterness. Forced to give up all their wealth, possessions, and comforts led the whole family to experience a lot of suffering and created a generation of families that struggled with basic survival, giving up everything except their pride, faith, and the rhetoric that somehow comforted her in her reminiscing of better times.

Pancho Villa, a Mexican bandido, known for being a murderer, bank robber, and cattle thief, became a folk hero for the poor Mexicans. Prior to 1910, he became a legendary hero to the poor Mexicans for skillfully evading the powerful oppressors of the times. His oppressors governed the wealthy. The poor indigenous population began to rebel. Villa, at the age of fifteen, became a sharecropper after his father died. He worked to support his mother and four siblings. He witnessed the rich becoming richer by taking advantage of the poor, many times treating them as slaves. He and his group of bandidos would steal cattle, rob shipments of money, and commit atrocities against the wealthy. Confiscating hundreds of estates from their owners known as hacendados, Papa

Grande and Mama Grande being one of many hacendados, Villa and other Mexican generals confiscated the haciendas and administered them for the poor, especially for widows and their children to live in as a reward of the revolution. He became a revolutionary leader after 1910, leading an army of thousands of men known as *la Division del Norte* army. The lower-class, poor field-worker and sharecropper Mexicans saw Villa as the modern-day Robin Hood hero of Mexico. During this revolutionary time, the Mexican government began to ask the wealthy hacendados to either contribute money toward the war effort or offer a son to serve in the Mexican army to help fight in the revolution. Neither option was acceptable for Papa Grande. Papa Grande told Mamá that his grandparents had migrated from Burgos, Spain, along with twenty-five other families to start a new life in Mexico. They brought with them all of the Spanish traditions and worked very hard to recreate a settlement very similar to the one they left behind in Spain, even naming the city that they developed Burgos. According to Mama Grande's story, the family fled as soon as they found out that their hacienda was going to be taken over by the Villistas. Papa Grande refused to give any of his sons to the revolutionary cause. Maybe that is why Tío Exiquio was never registered as crossing the border. Being the only son of age to serve in the military and fear that he may be forced to serve may have been the reason for not registering him at the border.

Los abuelos settled in Pharr, Texas, in the Rio Grande Valley just eleven miles north of the Rio Grande River, which is the line of demarcation dividing the United States from Mexico. Records show that Papa Grande Alejo bought one-half of lot 13, the west side, in block 14 of the original townsite of Pharr in the barrio. He paid $400 for a piece of land twenty-five feet wide and one hundred feet long in 1927. Ten years later, he bought the other half of lot 13, the east side, for only $10.00. I remember the dirt-floor hut that they had to live in before Papá and his brothers Tío Julian and Tío Lupe saved enough money working in the fields to build them a home in the front of the lot. The eldest brother,

Exiquio, left the family in pursuit of his own life, and the family did not hear from him for ten years. The home had a formal living room, dining room, kitchen, bathroom, and two bedrooms. All the furniture in the living room and dining room, covered with clear plastic to preserve its longevity, was upholstered in a rich burgundy color made of velveteen fabric. Material possessions were valued and cared for as if they were animate objects. We the grandchildren were never allowed to sit in the formal areas. We sat on the floor when we visited. I recall being about three years old, standing in the backyard of our house and seeing the chickens pecking away on their yard next to us. Mama Grande would have chicken feed in her hand and walk around the yard spreading it for the chickens to eat. I hated the sound of the roosters crowing so early in the morning. I always wanted quiet, especially in the mornings. I do not recall ever seeing Mama Grande smile or hearing any laughter from her. She never seemed to have accepted the fate of all her losses, but she survived it well to old age.

As I grew older, I wondered how the abuelos and Tía Julia survived financially. No one in that household worked, and no one spoke English. I learned later in life that Papá provided them with a $500 monthly allowance for survival. I suppose in the 1940s and 1950s that was ample amount of money for three adults to survive. The milk deliveryman delivered milk to our home for not only our family, but also for the abuelos' home. In addition, the milkman also delivered eggs many times. Sometimes Papá would order us to take the milk over to Mama Grande. The majority of the time, Loreto Jr., the firstborn son in our family, a year younger than I, would run over and deliver the milk to Mama Grande as Papá gave the order.

Loreto was never a big kid. Actually, he was a gangling, lanky-looking kid, very fair skinned with auburn hair, and had difficulty with his vision from the time he was a very young child. He had a very weak left eye that was very sensitive to sun exposure. He wore glasses before he was in the second grade. Papá and Mamá did everything they could to help him with the problem; I recall Papá buying an electric juicer to make carrot juice for Loreto Jr. to drink daily.

Loreto grew to dislike Tía Julia vehemently. He recalls a time when Tía Julia slapped him because he could not keep his eyes opened while speaking to her. A Treviño child with manners was supposed to listen to adults attentively when addressed and look at the adults attentively. An environment full of expectations that created mental and emotional stress on us daily surrounded us. We learned to respond to the environment by following instructions immediately or consequences followed. On one occasion, the milkman was late with his delivery; Loreto was in such a hurry to get the milk over to Mama Grande before eight in the morning that he fell down as he missed the entrance step to their home. He broke the glass milk bottle and severed his pinky. Tía Julia didn't even come over to help him. He ran home, and Mamá called Dr. Long to ask for help. Dr. Long was everyone's doctor in the barrio and made house calls, so he came over to take care of the stitching of the finger.

At the age of eighty-nine, Papa Grande fell down in the backyard of his home and broke a hip. Even though the family doctor said that he would be able to walk again after he healed, Papa Grande never walked again. Mama Grande, now at the age of seventy-four, would help with the cooking, but that was about it for housework. Tía Julia, Papá's oldest sister and the firstborn female of the family, was expected to take care of both her parents until their death. Papá Grande never allowed her to date, let alone wed. Mamá told me that from birth, her role was to care for her parents. She was faithful to her obligation, and Papa Grande lived three years bedridden until his death in September 11, 1956. Tía Julia had a very difficult role to fulfill, but she did it, many days looking exhausted and worn.

Papa Grande's death will remain imprinted in my mind forever. When the neighborhood found out about his death, all the neighbors started gathering in both our homes and brought food and more food. Within an hour of his death, a huge woman named Maria came into his home, leaned against the corner of the bedroom where he passed, placed her arm against her forehead, and very loudly cried out the *grito del duelo*, a very loud outcry of sorrow done sequentially three times. My sisters and I just stood there and watched, stunned! I learned later from Mamá that this was a way to inform the neighborhood that there had been a death in the home. We had a telephone line, but the majority of homes in the barrio did not have telephones in the 50s, so this was the traditional way of communicating that the family had begun the period of *luto* (mourning) for a year. An additional custom in announcing a death was in the printing of an *esquela*, a short notice in the form of a letter. The esquela was distributed by hand to all the homes in the neighborhood.

Yes, a full year of mourning, so the first thing my mother did the next day was to have Pablo, our handyman, drive her to the local department store to buy black and white material so she could make us all skirts and blouses to wear for a full year of mourning. Mamá did not know how to drive, another expectation of the culture. The man of the house took care of everything outside the home. Women were to stay home and go out only with their husbands. Yes, we had to wear black skirts and white blouses to school everyday to let everyone know we had lost a loved one in the family. In addition, we were not to watch TV or listen to any music or the radio for a full year.

Another tradition followed was that the deceased was honored with a wake (*velorio*) held in the living room of his home, his body exposed for a full twenty-four hours before the burial. No family member was to sleep during the night of the wake. It began with a Rosary said by the parish pastor, and then everyone took turns kneeling down in front of the casket and praying for his soul throughout the night. The grandchildren were ordered to go to bed after midnight. I recall seeing Tío Julian, Tío Lupe, and Papá kneeling in front of the casket kneeler, praying, and kissing Papa Grande's forehead several times during the evening.

Since I was one of the organists who could play the *Missa pro defunctis*, Papá told me that I was to play for the funeral Mass. This was the first time, at the age of twelve, I came to a realization what a Requiem Mass was really all about. I knew it was a Mass for the dead, but in all of the other masses I had played for, I had not had an emotional connection with the person who died. I was very fond of Papa Grande and had become accustomed to seeing him daily because it was customary for us to go visit with both grandparents and Tía Julia daily, ask about their well-being, and give them a good-night kiss. Prior to his fall, using his cane he would walk over to our home next door about midafternoon to join us for the traditional merienda. He always wore a jacket when he came to visit us, even in the heat of the summer. We would indulge in pan dulce and coffee or hot chocolate depending on the time of the year. Unlike Mama Grande, he was a soft-spoken man, always remaining calm regardless of what was happening anywhere. He was very tall, slim, fair skinned with green eyes, and projected a lot of character and class. He would chat with us about our schooling and events going on in the neighborhood. He repeatedly reminded me that I was his favorite *hijita* (little daughter) because the baptismal name given me was in memory of a daughter they had lost at the age of twenty-one. She became sickly in her late teens, and no one knew the exact cause of her death. According to the census records, she registered with the family as crossing the border on September 9, 1928, and the Texas Death Index shows her date of death as September 11, 1929. All the family raved about her having been the most beautiful of all the daughters.

Papa Grande's funeral was not like all the rest I had seen. During Mass, I went about my duties sometimes numb, realizing it was the last tribute for Papa Grande. After Mass, on our way to the cemetery, we got into Papa's car, and I saw a side of Papá that he never showed. Papá started sobbing like a child as we waited for the procession to form to go to the cemetery. What a shock to see Papá being so human and so emotionally connected to his papá. From that experience, I learned that in my family, contrary to the belief that Hispanic men do not ever cry, men do cry, and it is perfectly acceptable. The ceremony at the cemetery is as memorable as if it had happened yesterday. All of us grandchildren along with all of his children stood around the casket and watched it lowered very, very slowly to the bottom of the grave pit. Tears flowed uncontrollably. Why did we have to see the casket going down? That hurt. Then each one of us picked up a handful of dirt from the ground and sprinkled it on the casket before processing off the grounds.

Mamá did not attend the funeral because she had just given birth to Maria Del Rosario a month earlier on August 7. After giving birth, women had to take very good care of themselves for at least six weeks after the birth. They were not to be around crowds and stayed home to take care of themselves and the baby. The only outing for Mamá after the birth of a baby was to present the baby at church for a blessing and for Sunday Mass.

Several months after the funeral, mother convinced Papá that we were too young to continue wearing the black-and-white attire to school. She also believed depriving us from watching TV or listening to the radio was not good for our environment. We never went to the movies or socialized with anyone unless it was with the whole family at church functions or Knights of Columbus functions. Papá gave in and allowed us to drop the customs. Mamá Grande and Tía Julia never approved of us giving up the expected customs; the neighbors and family members heard their criticism of Mamá's influence on Papá for years.

Mama Grande only lived four more years after Papa Grande passed away. She suffered from gallbladder attacks, but Dr. Long did not want to do surgery because he believed she could not survive the anesthesia. He was right. During the summer of 1960, when Papá was in Lubbock with the usual migrant families that went to pick cotton for the summer, Mama Grande had an attack, and Tío Julian and Tío Lupe asked a doctor from McAllen to come to the house to check her. That doctor decided she needed surgery immediately. Wide-awake and alert, she was transported to the hospital in an ambulance. We watched her get in the ambulance. She asked the doctor in front of us if she was going to die. He said, "No senora."

She was prepared for surgery. She was given anesthesia and died before the doctor made any incision. The doctor concluded that she was allergic to the anesthesia. Dr. Long was right in his diagnosis of her not being able to handle the anesthesia because of her age. She was eighty-one years old. Papa drove back from Lubbock immediately for the funeral.

Papa Grande Alejo Trevino and Mama Grande Margarita Trevino Trevino

Mama Esperanza

To the woman he said,
"I will greatly increase your pangs in childbearing; in pain you shall
bring forth children, yet your desire shall be for your husband, and
he shall rule over you."
                                                    - Genesis 3:16

Mamá, Esperanza Pierro Fierros, always had a beautiful tan skin (*morena*) very typical of many Italians. Papa's family, being of very fair skin, with a lot of auburn hair and hazel green eyes, always claimed they came from pure European blueblood. As I grew older, it became obvious to me that the Treviño family members were very biased when it came to skin color. Even though Mamá was born in Brownsville, Texas, she practiced many of the same traditional European customs that Papá's family abided by. Nevertheless, it was evident that the elder Treviño women never approved of her. I concluded that because she was of Italian background, not Spanish, she never met their expectations of the ideal wife they envisioned for a son and brother. Mamá was educated at the Sacred Heart Catholic Elementary School with the Sisters of Mercy and finished high school with honors in the McAllen public schools.

Her biological parents, Luis Pierro III and Irene Fierros Pierro, resided in San Antonio, Texas, from the time Mamá was a baby until their death. Her great grandparents emigrated from Naples, Italy, via Mexico and settled in Brownsville, Texas, in the early 1900s.

Mama's life prior to marrying Papá was like a Shirley Temple movie. As a newborn, her parents, Luis Pierro and Irene Fierros, went on a visit to Monterrey to visit relatives and stopped to visit Mamá Irene's brother Juan Fierros Sr. and his wife Maria Del Rosario P. Fierros in McAllen, Texas. Juan Sr. had high blood pressure and was ailing with heart problems. His sister Irene felt it necessary to stop by, spend time with her brother, and introduce the newborn baby Esperanza to the family. The Fierros only had two children, Eva and Juan Jr., and they were already in their early twenties. This family size was very small for the era. As the story goes, Tío Juan Sr. and his wife Rosario immediately requested that baby Esperanza stay with them instead of taking her on the trip to Mexico where there was a high probability that the child would encounter a difficult environment. Tío Juan's family owned a Jersey farm, and there was always plenty of fresh milk for the baby. Grandma Irene had given birth to several sets of twins, but they only survived a few months. No one knew why the babies would not survive. Rafaela was Mama's only sister, about seven years older than she was. Papá Juan and Mamá Rosario also suggested to Mamá Irene that maybe they could help her with this baby by keeping her in the McAllen environment instead of San Antonio, "haber si se te logra" (to see if she could be saved).

Mamá shared many stories with me as I grew up. She explained that families thought nothing of helping with each other's children especially during an era when families faced many struggles and no answers as to why children did not survive. They bonded with the baby Esperanza (Hope) within the months that they begged to keep her. Mamá Irene and Papá Luis came back to get her several times but were never successful in taking her back to San Antonio. The excuse used was that Tio Juan would suffer another heart attack if the apple of his eye left him. He had encountered heart problems several years before, and he was now only in his early fifties. A few years later in 1921 Mamá Irene gave birth to Uncle Carlos and two years later in 1923 to Uncle Alex, both reared in San Antonio. Juan and Rosario Fierros legally adopted Mamá at the age of four, but she kept her biological birth last name of Pierro. Throughout her life, she visited San Antonio regularly to spend time with her parents, sister Rafaela, and brothers Carlos and Alex.

She was lavished with attention by the two older first cousins, Juan Jr. and Eva. She had a nanny, Tía Catalina, who helped in educating her in the role of a woman. She learned to cook, sew, embroider, can fruits and vegetables, and garden. She was formally educated with the Sisters of Mercy at Sacred Heart Elementary School and was a model student. Since there was no Catholic high school in McAllen, she attended a McAllen public high school. She graduated with honors at the age of seventeen. She was a kindergarten teacher at Sacred Heart Catholic School when Papá met her. She started teaching there after high school after the nuns had taught her the curriculum to teach. She loved teaching and taught for seven years before she was married.

The Treviño traditional belief was that women were to keep their hair long, preferably in braids, and wear no makeup; skirt lengths were to be ankle length, and groom your nails but no polish. Mama's hair was short and permed. She showed her ankles, wore makeup, and used light-colored nail polish. She always dressed in the latest dress styles, had danced with the Ballet Foklórico in the McAllen community theatre shows, and spoke both English and Spanish perfectly.

She did not project the image of a traditional Spanish señorita. She was also quite a homemaker, a great cook and seamstress, and was the family bookkeeper throughout their married life. She and Papá had known each other for seven years prior to their marriage. I always wondered why they took so long to decide to get married. She was twenty-four years old when she married, and during that era, she was already considered an old maid. For unknown reasons, Mamá never met the approval of Mamá Grande and Tía Julia. Papa Grande never demonstrated any disapproval verbally or otherwise. He enjoyed coming over and visiting with her. Mamá never showed any disrespect of any kind for them at any time, regardless of what they thought of her. Her level of tolerance and acceptance of her life was admirable. She modeled respect for all of Papa's family members at all times regardless of their behaviors. Traditionally, whatever hardships came with marrying into a family were to be tolerated and endured.

Since both of my parents had grown up adhering to many European customs and values, especially following the commandment of "honor your father and mother," questioning an elder's directives, beliefs, or wishes was never acceptable even in thought.

By the time I was in the eighth grade, Mamá was giving birth to her thirteenth child. They were married in 1941, and she had her first pregnancy in 1942. The first pregnancy resulted in a miscarriage. From 1943 to 1958, a period of fifteen years, she gave birth to eight girls and four boys. In 1949, the birth of a beautiful full-term baby boy, Juanito, was emotionally devastating when he did not survive a full twenty-four hours. She had already given birth to three girls and two boys, so having another boy was a blessing. The baby swallowed fluid during the birth. I was five years old, and I remember the wake and the burial. The wake was held in our living room with Juanito lying in a beautiful small white casket all cushioned with beautiful white satin. Baby Juanito was dressed in a beautiful white silk baptismal baby-boy outfit. Mamá always seemed to stay calm during difficult times. I saw her crying a lot during the wake, but she was not to view the baby all night because she had to take care of herself and rest.

Mama's life was totally dedicated to Papá and her children. She catered to Papá. She nurtured a male-dominant environment, and Papá and my brothers were to be taken care of first. We never sat down for dinner unless Papá was home to lead us as head of the household. Many evenings he would not come home until after seven, and we would all have to wait until he arrived before we could have our *cena* (dinner). As I grew older and watched every interaction between them, I could never get over how Papá would go into the bathroom to take a shower without taking any of his clothing. As he finished his bathing, he would yell at Mamá, "Viejita, tráeme la ropa." *Viejita* is a term of endearment used by many Spanish-speaking husbands to refer to their wives. Mamá would stop doing whatever she was doing, walk to their bedroom at the front of the house, gather his clothes, and take them to the bathroom at the other end of the house. As the years went by, I could see how exhausted she looked. Papá was unreasonably demanding of her attention, and he always came first.

Mamá was expected to not only take care of Papá, the children, and keep the house tidy, but also to stretch the budget and resources that Papá provided. Papá bought as much as he could wholesale. Whenever he had a good season financially, he would buy one hundred hens and have them delivered in cages to our backyard for slaughtering. Mamá started the process first by boiling huge aluminum tubs of water and having them ready for later. The next step was grabbing a chicken one at a time and twisting the chicken's neck and laying it on the ground until there was no more movement. Some of them put up a good fight and jumped endlessly. It scared me to death! The chicken was now ready to be soaked in the boiling water for just a few seconds so the feathers would be ready for plucking. Plucking of the feathers came next. I helped with that part. I was always amazed at how easy it was for the feathers to come off. Cleaning out all the guts was next. That was also part of my assignment. Then it was time to wash and rinse the chicken before covering it in foil for freezing.

The huge deep freezer inside the house in the room we called the *cuartito* (little room) located at the end of the house always had to be cleaned thoroughly before we started the slaughtering of the chickens. At least once a year Papá received a huge round piece of yucky-smelling white cheese from a priest in Spain. The odor was unbearable! The smell of the cheese overtook the freezer! How can any taste bud tolerate that kind of odor?

Sometimes it took two days to get all one hundred hens dressed. During these days, Mamá managed to prepare all the hens in addition to cooking meals for the family. This event was exhausting! We ate chicken every day at least once a day for either lunch or dinner for months.

Her only connection to the academic world was her continued interest in reading. The newspaper, delivered daily to our home, was her connection the outside world. She joined a Reader's Digest Book Club and received books by mail monthly. She discussed her readings with some of the women on the other side of town on the phone. They discussed the readings and the characters of the novels they read. I recall listening to her conversations after school. I don't think anyone of our neighbors in the barrio had any idea what a Reader's Digest Book Club was. She enjoyed reading novels. I suppose it was her escape from the enormous demands on her life as wife and mother. I do not know when she found the time to read with so much work to do, caring for Papá with all of his demands, the children, and all the household duties. Maybe she read while we were in school.

With the exception of the youngest child, Rosa, all of us were born at home. Dr. W. Long, a family practitioner, was our doctor all of our lives, and he came to the house to deliver all the babies. By the time Mamá was delivering her seventh child, she had developed very high blood pressure. In later years, I found out that she carried an inherited gene of hypertension, which eventually led to strokes. Her biological father passed away from a stroke at the age of sixty-three. Additionally, her adoptive father, who was also her biological uncle, passed away from a stroke before he was sixty. Dr. Long cautioned Papá to stay away from her and stop having babies. Papá never listened. They practiced the Catholic teaching of no artificial birth control of any kind. Eventually, she would suffer consequences.

Our next-door neighbor, Doña Adelina (known to all of us as "Comadre"), and Fina, an older Native American woman who lived in the alley in one of the two-room huts, were the midwives or *curanderas* of the barrio.

Fina, a very short woman, of leathery, wrinkly looking very dark skin, with no teeth, preferred to walk barefooted all over the neighborhood. We never knew of a husband, but she did have a daughter. Many times Papá would tease her about her walking into our home barefooted. Papá had a rule of not having anyone in the house walking barefoot especially in the kitchen or while serving food in the dining room. Papá would pay her wages to come and help Mamá especially after the birth of a baby. She was very poor, and many times, she would come over and help herself to whatever food we had in the house even if there was no work for her to do to earn it. Fina made the best flour tortillas in the neighborhood. Papá always had a heart for people in need, so sharing food with anyone in need was a practice that I saw time and time again.

Unlike Fina, Comadre, also a very short woman of Mexican Indian decent, did not have very dark skin. She always wore her very long hair pulled to the back, made into a very thick braid. She was soft-spoken and a great listener. She also had a large family but had a strong body that always looked healthy. She always struck me as being very philosophical and accepting of whatever life brought. She was a calming force to Mamá. Once time neared for Mama's delivery, Fina and Comadre would be on alert to come at a moment's notice. Mamá had the reputation of being a baby factory. She seemed to enjoy being pregnant and had a perfect body structure for carrying babies. Her labor never lasted more than three to four hours. Comadre and Fina prepared everything for Dr. Long. He would come and take care of the delivery to make sure all was normal. I recall going to school and coming home several times to find a newborn sibling in our household.

Mamá never relied on any family members to help her at any time. Her adoptive parents passed away before she was twenty, and her birth parents lived in San Antonio. Her father passed away of a heart attack at the age of sixty-three in 1944, the year I was born; and her mother passed away in 1950 at the age of sixty-five on February 9, a day after Mamá had given birth to her seventh child, Esperanza (Hopie), born a premature baby just a year after Baby Juanito had died. Mamá could not attend her funeral. Of her two brothers Carlos and Alex, Tío Alex was the closest to her. Both brothers served in the military during World War II, Tío Carlos in the army and Tío Alex in the navy.

About 1950, when I was six years old, Tío Alex came to live with us for a few months until he found a job. He had served in the USS *Copahee,* a naval carrier, during World War II. He was a cook and enjoyed demonstrating his cooking skills. He could crack two eggs with one hand at the same time and never break the yolk. I was fascinated watching him cracking eggs. I never learned how to do it! I recall when he cooked spaghetti sauce for family dinner. He started by nine in the morning and finished by six in the evening. The sauce simmered all day long. He monitored it by stirring regularly and tasting it for flavor, making sure the taste buds experienced the garlic and oregano.

Comadre and Fina were very much loved by all of our family. They were Mama's guardian angels. Comadre would check on Mamá daily and bring her special *platitos* of a bland diet that were the custom for after-birth care. For a full six weeks after giving birth, Comadre monitored her. She was an incredibly caring woman who lived in a home on the lot next to ours since before my parents were married. I do not recall ever seeing Tía Julia or Mama Grande checking on Mama's health or well-being.

Mama Irene Fierros Pierro and Papa Luis Pierro III

Mama Esperanza Pierro in downtown McAllen, TX 1938

Tio Carlos Pierro and Tio Alex Pierro

Mama and Papa on their wedding day, 1941

Papa Luis Pierro with Mama in San Antonio 1939

Papa

For I was hungry and you gave me food, I was thirsty and you gave me drink, I was a stranger and you made me welcome.
- Matthew 25: 35

Papá was adamant about not sending any of his children to public schools. He believed that all public schools students lacked respect for adults, and all boys attending public schools were interested only in seeing what they could get from the girls. The Catholic faith was the center of our family life, and the Catholic Church was the center of the social events and activities that were a safe haven for all families to attend. Papá would allow us to go to any church function as long as it was on church grounds just a block from our home.

When it was time to start high school, he decided to send my older sister Imelda and me to Villa Maria Academy, an all-girls high school led by the Sisters of the Incarnate Word in Brownsville, sixty miles away from home. I do not recall ever being asked if I wanted to go. We boarded with an aunt from my mother's side of the family, Tía Berta Colsa. Living with Tia Berta and her only daughter, Bertita, provided us an opportunity to live very differently. During the year that we went to school there, I was to do nothing except study and attend school functions. What a difference in expectations! I was used to being busy all the time—going to school, coming home and cooking for the whole family, helping Mamá with the housecleaning, doing homework, tutoring my younger sisters, and ironing all day Saturday. Tía had a live-in housecleaner that did all the housework. We would go home to visit our parents, siblings, and grandparents during Thanksgiving, Christmas, and Easter holidays. It was a major adjustment to be away from home at the age of fourteen, but it was also a great learning experience, having an exposure to a very different kind of family life. Tío Manolo, Tía Berta's husband, worked in Mexico City and came to visit on weekends often. We joined Tía and Bertita for the symphony and concerts. In addition, we could have boys over to the house for socials, always being chaperoned by Tía. Papá never knew that was allowed. We also went to Matamoros, across the river to Mexico, many times to shop for many grocery items that were far more economical there than in Brownsville. We never carried any official papers with us. We just answered the questions about citizenship that the Border Patrol officers asked.

On one occasion, an officer on the Mexican side of the border asked the usual question about citizenship. Where were you born? Are you a U.S. citizen? Tía answered that we were all American citizens, but the officer kept staring at me and responded that he did not believe that I was from the United States. He wanted me to get out of the car and go with him to be questioned. Tía Berta was furious! She questioned his reasoning for wanting to take a fourteen-year-old señorita for questioning. She sternly questioned him about having a hidden motive for wanting me to get out of the car. She raised her voice firmly and was on the verge of making a scene when he finally told us we could go on. I did not understand what was going on. Why did she make a big deal of this? On the way back home, she explained to us that many older men would do anything to take advantage of young señoritas. Being a "senorita" meant you were a virgin, and culturally, it was very important that a young woman remain a senorita until marriage. An honorable young man would not even consider marrying a young woman who had a reputation of not being a senorita. This was my first lesson in awareness of older men and their cunning behaviors.

Attending Villa Maria High School had a spiritual impact on me that has lasted a lifetime. After attending a Lenten weekend retreat, I made a conscious commitment to practice my Catholic faith for the rest of my life. I sincerely believe I truly learned to talk to God personally that weekend. Prior to that experience, rote prayers were the extent of my spiritual development. I have sincerely attempted to practice my faith knowing that it is a continuing effort with struggles and challenges that I will face until the end of life. The school culture was very different from St. Margaret School where families were poor. At Villa Maria, many of the girls came from well-to-do families and acted as if they were spoiled rotten. Some were loud, rambunctious, and very theatrical. Others struck me as being very demanding of things they wanted like a new car, transistor radios, record players, and all the latest 45-RPM records. I came from a family where there were greater needs to address than things to keep one entertained. We had television and radio to keep us entertained at home, and that was enough. The school year ended successfully academically, and I returned home with a much larger frame of reference than what I had prior to being there.

Rarely did Papá ever ask me for an opinion. At the end of the first year in high school, Papá asked me if I wanted to go back to Villa Maria for the rest of my high school years. I asked him to think about this seriously because if he expected Imelda and me to continue at that school, was he also expecting to send the rest of my sisters there when they finished the eighth grade? What impact would that have financially on the family budget? There were eight girls in the family, and the expense of tuition, room, and board was not a small sum of money for such a large family during that era. His work was seasonal and totally depended on the crops planted and the number of field-workers he could hire to go pick the crops.

He owned three working trucks and hired truck drivers to pick up the workers daily during each season. He had many very financially successful years during the forties and fifties being the *jefe* (boss) doing this work and learning all the details of the fruit and vegetable packing shed market, but income was unpredictable and fluctuated from month to month. He even owned a semi-pro baseball club that won the South Texas championship in 1947. Throughout the year, his income depended on the seasonal fruits and vegetables crops, cotton, and the weather. Annually, he would leave us at home with Mamá, and he would migrate with all three trucks full of migrants to the fields in Lubbock or even to Mississippi to pick cotton after the seasonal summer cotton crop was over in the Valley. In the fall and winter months, he worked with the Valley Fruit & Vegetable Company. During those seasons, the vegetable pickers picked lettuce, carrots, cabbage, beets, onions, cucumbers, radishes, turnips, tomatoes, oranges, and grapefruits. Everything depended on whether the Valley had had a good-enough rainfall for the crops to mature and yield enough crops for families to make a living financially.

We never went with him to any of these places, and we were forbidden to mingle with the workers. He told me many times that he wanted his children to have a better life than he ever had and to get the education he never had. I just listened to all the conversations about his work and watched as all the preparations for the trips took place. All three bright-red trucks had his full name, *Loreto G. Treviño*, fully printed on each cab door. The truck beds were covered with a heavy canvass that protected the families from the sun and rain. It was always very hot when they left, so the trucks, already full of families, would all gather in front of our home in the street by five in the morning for the last final details to review. All the workers called Papá "Don Loreto," a title of respect for men who had earned it. Papá never walked out of the house without his Stetson hat and freshly pressed khaki pants with a distinct pressed line down the middle of both legs. Ironing the pants was very hard work. Sometimes, when I helped mother with the ironing, it would take me more than twenty minutes to iron each one. The hat added height to his tall figure that always projected an air of being in total control. The families packed their own food for the day. Papá always worried about carrying enough wooden barrels full of water for everybody. Basic provisions were also carried: flour, lard, sugar, salt, coffee, rice, and beans. The trucks followed each other with Papá in the lead truck. He always left his car parked in the big four-car green aluminum garage at the back of the house with the entrance through the alley. Mamá did not drive, so it did not help us any to have a big Oldsmobile 98 car left behind. We always walked everywhere—to church, to school, to the Hanshaw's five and ten downtown, to the doctor's office, and to buy groceries.

The only migrant workers I knew were my first cousins from Tía Barbaritas's family. She was Papa's sister whose husband abandoned her and all their six children. Left to survive on their own in Reynosa, across the border in Mexico, they did not let any family member know about their circumstance. To be left in that situation was very embarrassing. "Divorce" was not a word that was part of our cultural vocabulary. Papá did not know for months about the situation. When he found out what happened, he went to Reynosa and brought the whole family to Pharr and found them a place to live several blocks further away from our home.

To my surprise, Papá actually listened to me when I posed all the questions about how he planned to handle our future education. At last, he agreed, reluctantly, to let Imelda and me attend public school for the first time as sophomores in the fall of 1959. That was quite a revelation not only for us as students, but also for Papá who had no idea how to deal with the secular environment of the public schools. Mamá had graduated from McAllen High School, so she was very familiar with the public school environment. Papá attended elementary and junior high public schools as a child but never went to high school. In later years, I realized the hardships he must have encountered associated with the era, the difficult times after the World Wars, the labeling of all people coming from Mexico, and the lack of educational support embedded in a system that did not value the education of Mexican immigrants. He remained in school for six years and then dropped out. Occasionally, he told stories of attending the elementary school called the Pharr Mexican

Ward School and always outdoing his classmates in math. He always remembered Mrs. Buell as being the principal and encouraging him to stay in school. Times were difficult, and children worked in the fields to help support the family financially. Survival was far more important than getting an education.

As stern and strict as Papá was, he did have an immense amount of empathy and a very benevolent nature about him. As I grew older, I realized that he had seen a lot of suffering as a child with the experience of having to leave their hacienda and estate in Burgos, Mexico. Many times, he would tell stories of how he was compelled to help people because that was the right thing to do. Papá taught me that sharing our blessings was very important. I remember many a *bracero* coming to our door with only the clothes on their backs and asking for work, any kind of work.

The *bracero* was a temporary contract laborer that came from Mexico to perform manual labor specifically in agriculture to harvest the seasonal crops. The program began in 1942 due to a demand for manual labor during World War II and lasted until 1964. Everyone in the barrio knew that Papá owned trucks and contracted with the farmers and packing sheds to hire people to go pick the crops during all the different seasons of the year. I learned that it was important to feed anyone who came to the door. Papa would command, "Viejita (as he referred to mom), prepárales arroz con frijoles, tortillas, lo que sea, a estos pobres hombres que no han comido en todo el día" (Old lady, fix some rice, beans, tortillas, or whatever is in the kitchen, these poor men have not eaten all day long). Of course, we all followed his commands.

There came a time when he decided that some of the braceros who needed a place to live in and cook could use the huge green aluminum garage in the back of the house. He decided to, not only install gas connections and set up a stove, but also to install showers so the *hombres* would have a place to stay and take care of their needs until they had enough money to find a place to live. He always talked about the hardships that families were going through and how the children needed to go to the doctor when they were sick . . . but there was no money . . . so he would hand them the money to go and take care of it. He repeatedly said, "Pobre gente" (Poor people). What a generous heart! I learned to feed anyone who comes to our home!

At times, your greatest strength can also become your greatest weakness. Papa's benevolent behaviors are a perfect example of that. In the midfifties, he began lending money to every family who came to him and asked him for help with groceries, medical bills, or utility bills. He and Mamá kept an alphabetized ledger of the names of the families who asked for money. Entries reflect from $2.00 to $1,824.53 loans for items like food, hospital bills, and one entry of a down payment for a 1953 Ford by a man from Mission. By the early sixties, he had loaned out over $60,000 to many families, and he never recovered the majority of it.

Pablo, a handyman, did many household chores that Papá never had time to do. He was a shy very slim dark-skinned man. He painted the outside of our home and our bedrooms, cleaned and organized the garage regularly, worked on the maintenance of the trucks, and even helped Mamá with the yard when she needed it. He was a very quiet, gentle man, and we had permission to speak to him because he spent a lot of time in the house fixing things. He finally built up enough courage to tell Papá that he had a *novia* (girlfriend) and that he wanted to marry her but did not have any money for a wedding. I heard Papá telling Mamá that they needed to help him with the wedding because otherwise he would not get married. That was it! Mamá planned the wedding, and the ceremony was held in our home with a justice of the peace presiding over the wedding. I did not understand why the wedding was not held in the church. Perhaps the couple had not been baptized in the Catholic Church. Nevertheless, I recall the bride in her long white dress and Pablo dressed in a black suit sitting in the sofa of our home as their relatives all came over to congratulate the newlyweds and enjoy the homemade meal reception, cake, and coffee that Papá and Mamá had prepared for them. I got sick from drinking too much soda!

As I grew older, I realized that the generation that experienced the Depression lived in fear daily of the possibility of having to go through that experience again. I recall as a very young child, maybe five or six years old, sitting in the backyard and watching Mamá and Papá store massive amounts of staples in the basement of the garage. Papá had a basement built in the west corner of the garage. This was uncommon in South Texas since it is not tornado country. Twenty-five-pound sacks full of flour, sugar, rice, beans, and coffee and boxes full of canned fruits and vegetables that Papá bought wholesale from Mauro Perez, the wholesale vendor from Mission, were stored there. I learned later in life that they felt they had to do that to prepare in case another war occurred or the possibility of another Great Depression or even in case of an atomic-bomb attack.

Papa's commitment to the Catholic faith was center to his life. An oblate priest, Fr. James Smith, from Kentucky, influenced him greatly. Fr. Smith was one of the many missionary priests that celebrated Mass on Sundays in Pharr before there was an established church there. He taught Papá and many of the young boys in the barrio how to swim and fish in the Rio Grande River. He also taught them catechism prayers and how to be altar servers. Fr. Smith, a six-foot-tall slim man always dressed in boots, was a cantankerous man who had the reputation of being a tough cowboylike man who tolerated very little. Papá had evidently met his match. Fr. Smith knew how to control Papa's temper, keep him calm, and tell him to cool it in a language that Papá understood. Fr. Smith was a frequent guest at our house, joining us for dinner every Thanksgiving and Christmas. Since he was from Kentucky and had no family in Texas, he visited us every opportunity he had.

Papá also had a very soft spot in his heart for children. I recall watching him play with my baby sisters every time he had a few minutes after dinner. He was a hugger and believed in giving babies many kisses.

I recall seeing him smothering my younger sisters—Hopie, Margarita, Irene, Maria, and Rosa—with playful kisses all over their cheeks and throwing them up in the air playfully as Mamá watched him and asked him to stop for fear that they may be hurt. "No se hace nada," (nothing will happen) would be his reply. I learned that hugging was a healthy gesture that demonstrated affection, caring, and acceptance. Consequently, I have always been a hugger.

Pharr Semi-Pro Baseball Team 1947

Papa in 1939

Governor of Texas, Price Daniel, and Papa

Eleven Blessings—Los Hermanos

How is it possible for two parents to give birth to eleven distinctly different personalities? I suppose the answer lies with the experts who study genetics. My older sister Imelda is fifteen years older than my youngest sister Rosa Maria is. The way our family evolved seems to be like two families divided by the birth of the first five children beginning in August 1943 with Imelda de Jesus, me (Maria Del Carmen) in September 1944, Loreto Guadalupe Jr. in December 1945, Teresa in January1947, and Luis born in January 1948. Then the second part of the family began in February 1950 with Esperanza, Margarita in February 1951, Irene in October 1952, Enrique in October 1953, Maria Del Rosario in August 1956, and Rosa Maria born in January of 1958.

Imelda, the oldest, is the very *güera* of the family, just like Papa's side of the family—pale white skin, auburn hair, and very light brown eyes. She was always Papa's favorite; and we, the other ten children, always knew she was the "queen." She and I always shared a bedroom, and I never knew if she was going to get out of bed in a mood to speak or remain silent all day. Mama's excuse for Imelda's bad moods was always the same: "Amaneció de mal humor, no le hagas caso" (She woke up in a bad mood, pay no attention to her). By the time we were in high school, I learned to just wait and see if she would speak to me after I greeted her with a "good morning." Many days she would not even acknowledge that I was in the room. I learned to accept it as just part of her personality. I also learned to accept that she never helped in the kitchen with the cooking, baking, or washing dishes. She helped with the housecleaning on Saturday mornings if she didn't have to study. Why were expectations different for her than for me? I have yet to figure that out. I suppose because she was the oldest, the güera, and Papa's favorite.

When I was born with light skin and jet-black hair, I looked more like Mama's side of the family. However, since I was christened Maria Del Carmen, for a daughter that Papa Grande and Mama Grande lost as a teenager to an unknown cause, I became Papa Grande's favorite granddaughter. All of Papa's side of the family always accepted me because I was not dark-skinned, and I was a living reminder of a lost child. With Mama's side of the family I was know as *la consentida* (the favorite one) because I resembled their side of the family.

The pride and joy of a Hispanic father is always the birth of the firstborn son. Loreto Jr., born on December 12, was given his middle name, Guadalupe, in honor of Our Lady of Guadalupe whose feast is celebrated on his birthday. He also is very light skinned like Papa's side of the family. He and Luis, the fifth born and second son, managed to get themselves in trouble a lot during their growing years. Teresa—the most extrovert of our family, the fourth born, and also a light-skinned brunette—was lost between the two brothers and managed to get attention with her incredible talkative, extrovert personality. Luis, the light-skinned brunette who looked like Sal Mineo, would tan in summer months, learned to follow Loreto Jr., and managed to get himself in trouble regularly.

Like most boys, Loreto and Luis had slingshots and BB guns to play with when they were about seven or eight years old. Sometimes they used marbles as the ammo when using the slingshot. Luis was the marble player; at one time, he had accumulated one thousand marbles from winning many games with the neighborhood kids. One afternoon they decided to use the slingshot, using marbles, to target a prized rooster that our next-door neighbor Don Tomas, Comadre's husband, owned. Don Tomas had roosters that he used for cockfights. The rooster roamed around in the backyard, and Luis dared Loreto to hit it, taunting him with "I know you can't do it." Of course, Loreto was not about to let the dare go. He positioned himself, picked a prized marble, and, much to his surprise, hit the rooster perfectly in the middle of the head between the two eyes. Big mistake! Don Tomas was outside in his backyard, saw the event, and started blurting out obscene words, including warning them of what would happen when Papá got home. Sure enough, when Papá got home, Don Tomas related the incident to Papá, and in front of Don Tomas, they got a severe whipping with the belt and had to kneel down outside for the rest of the afternoon. Papa's whippings had to hurt because he was a big man with a very strong arm.

On another afternoon, they decided to play with their BB guns. Standing in front of one of Papa's trucks parked in front of the house, they decided to use cars driving through the street as targets for shooting. They kept shooting at the cars as they drove by, not realizing that one of the cars kept coming back around the block. It just so happened that that car had a police officer riding in the backseat. Finally, the car decides to stop, and out comes the officer.

The officer approaches the boys and asks, "What are you doing?"

Their response was simply, "Just playing with our BB guns."

"Where is your Papá?"

"He's at work."

"When will he be back?"

"In just a little while."

"All right, I'll sit right here on the porch with both of you until he gets home so I can tell him what you did." The officer sat in the front porch with both Loreto and Luis by his side until Papá got home.

As soon as Papa arrives, he asked the officer, "¿Qué pasa?" The officer explained to him what the boys were doing; and, of course, Papá took care of it immediately. He took off his belt, right there in front of the officer, on our front porch, and proceeded to whip both of them. I saw this from the living room door and ran to my room to cry. I always felt the hurt for them. I hated seeing anyone getting hurt and decided at a very early age that corporal punishment was something I would never use as a form of punishment on anyone. In addition to the whipping, the boys had to kneel down in Papa's bedroom for thirty days in a row, three hours each day after dinner. That punishment was a farce, since young minds will always figure out a way to minimize their misfortune. As soon as the boys went into the bedroom to kneel down, Papá would close the door and go to the living room to watch TV. I found out later that they sat on the floor as soon as the door closed. They went back to the kneeling position as soon as they heard Papa's heavy footsteps headed for the bedroom. There are advantages to having hardwood floors! It worked for them!

Loreto went to the oblate seminary, in San Antonio, to consider studying for the priesthood at the end of his eighth-grade year. His exposure to the seminary life sheltered him from other experiences that he would have otherwise experienced had he remained in Pharr going to public school, as Luis did. Luis got the brunt of Papa's demanding personality and expectations during the three years that Loreto was in the seminary. During the summer months, both of them had to go pick cotton with the rest of the workers Papá hired. Papá always told them they had to learn what it was like to work in the fields so they would decide to get an education instead of doing backbreaking work in ninety-eight-degree weather earning only a few dollars a day. We, the daughters, not allowed to do any kind of fieldwork or mingle with the workers, were to help Mamá at home and act like senoritas at all times. We never wore pants and shorts, rode bicycles, nor learned how to swim. Papá was not going to have any of his daughters be seen in bathing suits. We did not go out in public without wearing socks or stockings. Señoritas did not wear red, drink beer, or smoke. Only *cantineras* (bar maids) indulged in those types of behaviors.

Since Juanito was born and passed away within a twenty-four-hour period, there was a gap between Luis and the birth of Esperanza (Hopi) in 1950. Hopie was born a very tiny baby, weighing about five pounds. She became my baby play doll. I helped Mamá with Hopie all the time. I changed her diapers, fed her, and tried to teach her all the sounds used in speaking. A year later, Margarita was born, and Hopie was still neither crawling nor walking. Mamá consulted with Dr. Long regularly, and he decided to start testing Hopi to see if there was anything wrong with her. The only test available in the early fifties was a spinal-fluid test that determined if the child was going to be mentally handicapped. The test performed indicated that Hopi was a slow developer and would probably not live to be more than thirty-five years old. Mamá and Papá just accepted the news the best they knew how and continued with their lives as usual. At the age of two, Hopie was still not walking even though Papá had bought her a walker, which helped babies learn to walk faster. That didn't help her speed up her progress. When Irene was born in October of 1952, Hopi was already more than two and a half years old and still not walking. Teresa, Luis, and I tried to help her every way we could to get her to take a few steps by herself, reaching out to her with both of our hands, holding her by the waistline to provide her support, and supporting her under her armpits while pushing her ever so gently forward, all to no avail. Mamá always made each baby a silk pillow, so Hopi had her own pillow that she kept with her all the time. After her third birthday, one day while I was repeating the same techniques in the living-room floor in front of all of us, I decided to give her the pillow and have her hug it in front, as if it were a stuffed toy. She hugged the pillow and all of a sudden began walking toward me. Oh my God! What a beautiful welcomed sight! All of us in the living room began cheering her on. "Yes, Hopi, you did it! C'mon you can do it again." She did! Since that day, at the age of three, she began walking more and more; and we knew that even though she may be a slow developer, she was going to be fine because if she learned how to walk, then she could continue to learn even if it was at a slow pace.

Like all other children, Hopie entered school with the nuns at the age of five. I was in the fifth grade and took it upon myself to tutor her every evening. I liked playing teacher, and she was very pleasant about letting me do it. I just did what I could, reviewing the alphabet, numbers, and eventually the addition tables. Within the next two years, I realized that she learned everything I reviewed with her for the day. However, the nuns told us she could not do the work at school. One day I decided to test her in the morning before she left for school to see if she remembered the addition tables that she studied the night before. She forgot completely what she learned the day before. There was no such thing as special education classes in the early fifties, so Hopi's education became very limited when several of the nuns admitted to Mamá that they did not know how to help her learn. The nuns did the best they could. She remained in school until the eighth grade, just trying to do the best she could, even though we all knew she was never on level academically. I decided that I wanted to be a teacher to see if I could help kids learn.

I still do not understand how a person can be mentally handicapped, learn two languages, and retain enough vocabulary to relate a story in Spanish, after seeing it on TV in English. How could she learn to do all types of household chores like cooking, using a detailed process of sautéing, browning, adding flavorings, and simmering food until done, and not be able to do math, spell, or read paragraphs (only words randomly)? Hopi is amazing; now at the age of sixty, she still cooks for herself and manages to take care of household chores like washing, ironing, and cleaning. The brain is an incredibly complex learning organ. So much for the medical predictions of her only living to be only thirty-five!

With the exception of Maria Del Rosario—born in August of 1956, before school started—my younger siblings were born during the school year when I was in school. I was almost twelve years old and at an age when I was aware of everything around me. I managed to get to the kitchen, having a direct view of the bedroom, to watch what I could. When it was time for the baby to be born, Fina and Comadre came over and asked all of us children to stay in the living room because they had to take care of our mother. I only saw them preparing for the delivery by laying several sheets on the bed on top of newspapers where Mamá was to deliver the baby. They also gathered clean old towels and had newspapers on the floor. Mamá never moaned, cried, or screamed. Dr. Long came in; walked through the living room, dining room, kitchen, and to the bedroom where Mamá was; and delivered the baby. He was always worried about her very high blood pressure. He said, "I almost didn't get here on time. You are fast!" I think she was crowning by the time the doctor got there. Maria was the biggest baby Mamá delivered. She weighed eight pounds. She was a beautiful baby, with very light skin, jet-black hair, and huge black eyes. She was named after Mama's adoptive mother and biological aunt. She still has the most expressive eyes of anyone in our family.

Of the last five siblings, only two more were born güeros, Margarita and Enrique. Margarita, named after Mama Grande, became Tía Julia's favorite. Enrique, the incredibly talented musician, never really connected with Papa's family. He grew up surrounded by sisters and immersed himself in his studies and music. Irene, named after Mama's biological mother, has also very light skin, dark hair, and dark eyes. On several occasions, about the age of two or three, she would start crying for whatever reason, hold her breath, and turn purple. Mamá was terrified the first time Irene did this, so she called Dr. Long to find out what was wrong. Mamá even took her to the doctor's office to get her checked to make sure nothing was wrong. Dr. Long checked her and said, "She's throwing a temper tantrum. Next time this happens, just leave her alone.

She will breathe again when she decides to breathe." I panicked every time I saw her doing this and screamed, "Mamá, Mamá, Irene is turning purple again!" Reluctantly, I learned to leave her alone and not pick her up. She always managed to start breathing again.

Rosa Maria, the youngest, was the only one born in a hospital in San Juan. Mama's blood pressure was dangerously high, and Dr. Long worried that she may have complications because she was delivering a baby at the age of forty-three. At least Mamá got to stay in the hospital three days and got some rest. Rosa Maria looked just like Mamá—tanned skin, very slim frame, very dark hair and eyes. She also became our baby doll, and all of us carried her all the time. Poor Rosie, she must have gotten tired of being held all the time!

First Communion Imelda and I in May of 1951

Loretto (Lee) and Luis in 1965

Dias de Fiesta

We celebrated birthdays very simply by attending Mass and thanking God for another year of life and later in the day with homemade cake, candles, and ice cream. The best cake ever was the basic 1234 cake recipe made with real butter and extra vanilla. Ahh! The aroma of vanilla is what home baking is all about!

I recall having only one very small birthday party when I turned thirteen at the beginning of my eighth-grade year. I invited four of my school friends to join me for cake and ice cream. I felt so special. I was not used to getting attention at home. I took care of others, especially Papá and my younger brothers and sisters. It was fun having a small group of girls my age over for just talking.

When I was about six, Papá, along with Mamá, drove all five of us children—Imelda, Loreto Jr., Teresa, Luis, and me—to Montemorelos, in the state of Nuevo Leon, Mexico, to visit a couple of our tíos, Tío Enrique Treviño and Tío Rodrigo Treviño, who lived there. We stayed with Tío Enrique several nights. They were both owners of large ranches and farmland and lived in big homes designed around a squarelike plaza with many colorful plants and tropical trees. Every room in the house had an exit door to the *placita*, even the kitchen. Getting there took most of the day. By the time we arrived, we were exhausted. Mamá carried Luisito on her lap during all the drive while the rest of us sat in the backseat of the Oldsmobile. Tío Enrique had two daughters and a son already in their twenties. I was impressed just watching the girls. They did nothing. The servants took care of every need. The servants took them their clothing for changing, cooked all their meals, and even combed their hair. I stared, as all this seemed to me as if I was watching something on a TV show. I wondered why my cousins who lived in Mexico did not do things for themselves.

We celebrated Thanksgiving the way all Americans celebrate it. Mamá baked a turkey along with all the side dishes, stuffing, gravy, green beans, candied yams, cranberry sauce, fruit salad, and pumpkin pie with whipped cream. I rarely watched the parade on TV because Mamá always needed help in the kitchen with the cooking. The only Mexican dessert that we had for Thanksgiving was *empanadas*, a turnover made of sweet dough bread spiced with anise and cinnamon and stuffed with a sweet paste made of pumpkin and sweet spices.

Christmas was a very busy time. The kitchen was the center of my life. I enjoyed baking, so I baked every imaginable cookie I could as long as the ingredients were accessible in the kitchen. Teresa, my sister two years younger than me, and I learned how to bake sweet yeast breads, kneading the dough; rolling it; adding raisins, cinnamon, and dried fruits with red and green cherries; and watching it rise to double its size before baking. We spend hours in the kitchen baking. During my years at home, Imelda, my older sister, never liked to cook, so she was never around when the kitchen summoned help. We prepared for Christmas by baking many American breads and cookies, and Mamá always made tamales. I helped her with the tamales from the time I was twelve years old.

To make tamales requires an exhausting, labor-intensive all-day process, and by late afternoon, my back throbbed with pain from the continuous repetition of spreading the husks with the masa. We always had a live Christmas tree decorated with multicolored glass ornaments and lots of silver tinsel. Of course, the center of decorations was the manger waiting for the baby Jesus to arrive. Mamá and Papá did not make a big deal of the material gift giving for Christmas because they always told us that the real Christmas came when the three Magi visited Jesus on January 6 and shared their gifts with Him. Therefore, we each received a new outfit to wear along with new shoes and loads of candy for everybody. Mamá made most of our clothes, so that was one more job she added to her list of things to do before Christmas day. I do recall getting a medical kit, dolls, paper dolls, and a tricycle before I was seven years old. With the family growing every year, our Christmas centered on Midnight Mass, sharing sweets and tamales after Mass and enjoying visits from family members.

El barrio celebrated New Year's Eve with firecrackers and shooting bullets into the air at the stroke of midnight. Mamá always told us that it was a ridiculous way to celebrate, and she taught us to be scared because we never knew if a crazy drunk man would end up shooting himself instead of aiming into the sky. We were never allowed to go outside the house during New Year's Eve. Instead, we stayed inside and watched Mama make buñuelos, a very thin sugar cookie that is traditionally eaten on New Year's Eve for good luck. Mamá had a special recipe that her nanny used, and she very proudly explained to me that the cookies needed stretching to a very, very thin round circle to create a quality cookie. She told me that Tía Catalina, her nanny, had a special silk pillow that she used to stretch each cookie individually to create the perfect buñuelo. She taught me how to make them, and I still follow that tradition annually.

Personally, the best holiday to celebrate with all the family was Easter. Of course, we followed the fasting and abstinence rules of the church and prepared for Holy Week all during Lent. At school, I learned to play the entire accompaniment for the Holy Thursday Mass of the Last Supper, the Passion and Stations of the Cross for Good Friday, and the Easter Vigil for Holy Saturday services. Easter Sunday was a day when Papá forgot his role as our father and allowed us to tease him and crack *cascarones* on his bald head all afternoon long.

We started preparing for the event months in advance. Since we ate eggs for breakfast daily, Mamá started collecting the eggshells by cracking a small hole in the center of the eggs, pouring it out onto the pan for scrambled eggs, and rinsing the shells immediately. She did this every day for weeks. We always had at least twelve to fifteen dozen eggs to play with for Easter Sunday. Mamá used her teaching skills to teach us how to prepare them. About a week before Easter, we gathered around the dining room table and started coloring the eggs very meticulously using crayons. We had to be careful not to use too much pressure while coloring them or else they would crack. We used our school crayons and used whatever artistic talent we had to decorate, as we liked. We then filled them with confetti that we made ourselves by cutting little pieces of construction paper and covered the hole in the center with cutout circles of tissue paper using glue that we made with just a little flour and water. It was always a great family project, and the best part was to see Papá running as fast as he could so we could not catch him to crack the eggs on his head. His laughter was contagious! He pretended to start running away from you, then without notice, he would stop in a second and bend over so we could reach his head. Papá was an intimidating huge six-foot man weighing about 250 pounds, so reaching his head would have been impossible unless he bend over. He loved every minute of it and acted like a kid! Papá barbequed chicken on the grill; and as soon as the food was eaten, about midafternoon, the celebration would start. Loreto Jr. and Luis, my brothers, got a little wild during this time, being as rough as they could with Papá. This was the only day that I recall when none of us had to worry about Papá scolding us for every move we made or did not make. He forgot about parenting and enjoyed the event as much as we did. Mamá just enjoyed watching us enjoy the afternoon.

PSJA High School

Oh, the Brats . . .
Our youth now loves luxury. They have bad manners, contempt
for authority. They show disrespect for elders and love to chatter in
places of exercise. Children are now tyrants, not the servants of the
household. They no longer rise when elders enter the room. They
contradict their parents, chatter before company, gobble up their
food and tyrannize the teachers . . .

-Socrates

My first week in public high was as if I was walking into a foreign world, with far more students than I had ever seen assembled before. There was no busing service to our side of town, so we had to walk two miles each way to get to the old high school located on Highway 83 going east toward San Juan. During my sophomore and junior high school years, my sister Imelda and I walked to school daily. A group of us, about five or six of the neighborhood students, gathered at the corner every morning to start our school day. We also met in front of the school at the end of the school day to walk back home together.

On the first day of school, I embarrassed myself when an adult walked into one of my classes and I stood up. The teacher was very nice and asked me to sit down as all heads turned toward me to see what was happening. She informed me she knew that I had come from a private school and that in public school students did not stand up when an adult entered the room. Acknowledging when an adult entered a room was the respectful action to take. I thought it was very rude for students not to stand upon their arrival. First lesson in survival: observe other students' behaviors and learn how those behaviors were so different from Catholic-school expectations.

I carried my sandwich lunch daily; and on the first day, I went into the cafeteria, found it to be too loud and crowded, so I decided I was not going to eat there ever again. I found a spot on the stairs between the cafeteria and the next building, and that became my eating spot for the rest of the year. Sometimes Imelda would join me; but many times, I ate alone, for a full semester. By the second semester, I met a couple of girlfriends who also did not like the cafeteria atmosphere, so they joined me daily.

I have never forgotten Papa's reaction when he learned that we had to wear shorts to physical education class and that the boys were in an adjacent gym. Need I mention that his choice of vocabulary was more like that of a sailor than that of a devout practicing Catholic? He was ready to go to the school and tell that PE teacher in so many four-letter words that his daughters would do no such thing as wear short shorts in front of all the boys. Mrs. Cain, the PE teacher, asked daily for a week why I did not have my PE uniform ready for class. I explained to her that Papá did not want me wearing shorts in front of everybody. She was puzzled at my response and told me she did not understand why he thought that way. She was a huge woman who had been a wrestler, had a very attractive face, and had very expressive green eyes. She just nodded her head every time and grumbled, "I don't understand why your father thinks that way." She met with him at one point to calm down his concerns, but he was not convinced she was being truthful. Somehow, Mamá convinced him that we had to do what the school required in order for us to continue our education. Again, two weeks later, he reluctantly agreed that we could order the shorts for PE class.

Papá embarrassed me with his behavior, and I learned to apologize for him beginning with my high school years. As I continued to learn Papá's reaction to the public-school world, I also learned not to share with him many details . . . like having to shower in the gang showers in the gym. In addition were my many observations as to how rude so many of the students were with their behaviors, let alone share with him that some boys would even try to hug you in the hall while changing classes. I continued surviving, slowly learning the new system, and using my introversion, just like a fly on the wall taking it all in. I did learn to use my elbow quite effectively when boys got too close to me. I also quit eating by the stairs at the end of my sophomore year when I received a letter from an upperclassman informing me that he was going to marry me. I had several conversations with him because he also ate there, but I had no idea he felt that way about me. I thought I was just being nice and polite! I showed Mamá the letter, and her only comment was, "Esta loco (He is crazy)! Just stop talking to him." I had to find another place to eat to avoid this from happening again. I did!

The unwritten home rules enforced were quite simple. Go to church, go to school, study, do your homework, help Mamá, absolutely no boyfriends at any time, and no phone calls from boys. At least twice a week Papá would call Imelda (my older sister) and me into his bedroom for a talk. In reality, it was more of a lecture than a talk. "Siéntense," the order to sit down on the bed while he sat in his chair, always came first. The lecture was always the same. "Mis hijitas, tienen que educarse porque no saben con cual cabrón se van a casar (My dear little daughters, you have to get an education because you never know which bastard you will end up marrying). Look at what happened to your Tía Barbarita. She married that bastard who deserted her and left her with six starving children until I found out about it and went to rescue them from Reynosa, Mexico, and brought all of them over here to Pharr so that they could have a life."

Yes, Papá did do that, and he set them up in a small home a few blocks from where we lived. I remember meeting all my cousins and visiting with all six of them every Sunday afternoon. It was a tradition to spend Sunday afternoons visiting with Papa's brothers and sisters. All of them and their offspring would come to visit Mama Grande and Papa Grande weekly and inform them as to the events of the past week. Since we lived next door, we would watch for the first car to arrive, which was our cue to go for the visit. His nieces greeted Papá with a kiss on his hand, just as if you were greeting a pope. I even remember when my older female cousins had decided they were ready for marriage; the boyfriend would have to be introduced to Mama Grande and Papa Grande for approval prior to the approval given by the parents of the bride. In addition, on the day of the wedding, the bride (being the granddaughter) would have to visit Mama Grande all dressed in her wedding gown prior to going to church. It was a tradition that the grandparents would have to give the first blessing to the bride. Customs were very, very important in our family. Every morning we would go to the grandparents' home as we walked to school, and we had to greet them with an *abrazos, besitos,* and "Buenos Dias, Cómo amaneció?" (Good morning, how did the morning greet you?) In addition, in the early evening we would go by to say, "Buenas noches. Que Dios los bendiga" (Good night. May God bless you).

Greeting everyone (adults) we saw was also an expectation, and if you did not greet everyone whom you met in the barrio, the parents would hear about it before the end of the day. They were told how rude their children were. If that happened, we would get a verbal scolding and be told to correct our behavior. We greeted all adults who entered our home with an abrazo and besito, especially relatives. After all, we were reminded, we were not animals living in the wilderness.

As I immersed myself in my high-school career, I could attend a school function only if it was necessary for a grade. With all the rules in place, I quickly learned that the only way I could attend any school functions was if I got involved with clubs and organizations.

I became very active in Future Homemakers of America and Future Teachers of America. In addition to playing the organ at church for high masses during the week and, of course, for Sunday Mass, I was involved in the Catholic Youth Organization. Within a year, I was an officer in all three organizations and kept quite busy all the time. This very functional strategy helped me survive a never-ending controlling environment. Little did I know that this became a pattern as to how I was going to live the rest of my life!

I began to notice how so many of my Anglo-American friends would be dating and socializing with boys. They would talk to me about going to the drive-in movies, bowling, and to all the sock hops sponsored at school. Many of them were also driving by the time they were juniors in high school. I would not dream of asking to go to any of those types of social events—let alone asking if I could drive. Papá would never allow his daughters to be involved in any activities where boys could have the opportunity to take advantage of them. He practiced daily the preaching of "lead us not into temptation." In my mind, I always wondered why. Are we not living in America? Are not these American customs what we are supposed to be following?

Now, immersed in an educational setting with Anglo-American norms during school hours, I go home after school daily, shifting to rules, expectations, and customs of the European Spanish-Italian norms as our parents dictated. I never questioned anything verbally; I just did a lot of thinking and wondering. Questioning Papa's beliefs or authority was never an option. Papá also reminded us of the commandment, "Obey thy father and thy mother." He reminded us that he obeyed his parents until the day they died. Mamá was a lot easier to talk to, and I did ask her many times why did Papá believe the way he did. She just reiterated that his parents, who lived next door to us, set the rules and norms, and they deserved our respect.

I rarely encountered any problems academically with any of my courses. I needed an elective course as a senior to graduate. I decided to take theatre arts class. I had no idea what it involved. That was the worst decision I ever made! My teacher tried and tried to get me to understand that I was supposed to do, to ACT, the part that she had assigned me. I never got it! I was a lousy actress, not able to get into character or pretend I was someone else. I passed the class by becoming part of the stage crew.

By the time I was in my senior year in high school, I mustered enough courage to ask permission to go to a couple of evening functions that were sponsored by the FHA and FTA. After all, I always got good grades. I was never a straight-A student, but I made more As than Bs. I tried very hard to live up to my parents' expectations, especially the "obedience" part. Mama's recommendation was always to ask Papá for permission.

I knew his immediate response would always be a firm no. "No tienen ningún negocio andar fuera de la casa en la noche" (You have no business outside the house at night). Then Mamá would say, "Let him vent and brew for a day or two. He will change his mind in a few days."

What she never shared with me was that she would have a talk with him and help him understand why he needed to let us go to school functions. I even overheard some of those types of conversations because our bedroom was next to theirs, and I was able to hear many, many conversations they had in the early evenings. This was the beginning of my learning what the power of persuasion meant. Sure enough, a day or two after my initial permission request, Papá would call me to his room, and the interrogation began.

"Why do you want to go to that event?" "Papá, it's part of what the clubs do at school." "Is it part of a class project?" "Yes, Papa, it is."

"If that's what you have to do, then you and Imelda may go," was his response.

Then he would let us go . . . of course he would drive us and pick us up. Yes, my older sister Imelda and I had to do everything together even if we did not want to. (We were and still are as different as day and night.)

There was another rule: a young woman never went out of the house alone, and I did not until my college years when choices were limited because of class schedules. Actually, I got to a point where I never wanted to walk to school, church, or downtown by myself. I learned to be scared of the unknown. Inevitably, every time I'd walk somewhere, there were always a bunch of guys (*vatos*) hanging out at the corners, always ready to make comments like "oye chula" or "mamacita" or the traditional whistle that supposedly meant you were "good looking." For unknown reasons, I never considered all those comments or whistles as compliments. I suppose in the recesses of my mind I must have listened to all those lectures from Papá about the boys having other intentions. I learned to be cautious as I walked back and forth to church, school, or downtown. I created my own rule of never having direct eye contact with any of those compliment-giving *vatos*. I walked as fast as I could. Those types of behaviors embarrassed me. The rules of being courteous and using the greetings that were norms within the culture were not applicable here. However, as time went on, I thank God my parents were blessed with many children; otherwise, I would have never been allowed to leave the house or continue with life's journey, which is so needed to be travelled to reach a sense of independence and accomplishment.

Senior Memories

Forget Me Not
Today is a day for love and life,
And to forget of all the bloodshed and strife.
The clouds are fluffy, The sky is blue,
The sun shines brightly, just for you.
The birds sing softly as they go on their way, And in my heart you
shall always stay.
Cause if time comes that we must part,
I shall always have these memories deep in my heart.
- David Stoudt+
January 1944-April 1968

My senior year (1961-62) in high school was very active and memorable. I was an officer in the Future Teachers of America, president of the Future Homemakers of America, and won first place in the annual school style show. As the first-place winner, I represented PSJA High School at the FHA state-level style show in Dallas. I thought Papá was never going to allow me to go to Dallas to represent the school. I worried all the time. The two teacher sponsors, Mrs. Magueghy and Mrs. Norton, asked me if they could come over to the house to meet with Papá and Mamá to discuss all the details of the trip to Dallas. I explained to Papá that my teachers wanted to come to speak to him about a trip that they wanted me to go to, to represent the high school. Mamá was very proud that I was the only one asked to represent the school. She explained to Papá that I would be the only student representing all the home economics classes at the state level.

Both Mrs. Magueghy and Mrs. Norton came to the house after school. I had prepared cookies to serve them. Papá was very polite and cordial with them and granted me permission for the trip. He was impressed that I was going to have two chaperones taking care of me. I was thrilled! This was the first time I was allowed to go somewhere without a parent, brother, or sister.

This experience, driving to Dallas with my teacher sponsors, was my first experience (at the age of seventeen) learning what being labeled "Mexican" was and what prejudice meant. Mrs. Magueghy took me aside prior to leaving for the car trip to Dallas from Pharr, a twelve-hour drive. She instructed me that we would be stopping for lunch at a restaurant on the way; I was to stay with them at all times because there were eating places that refused service to certain people, and they did not want that to happen to me. What did she mean "refuse service to certain people"? I was to do as they said and not talk to any of the servers. This was not a difficult task for me since I always preferred observing rather than getting involved in conversations. I suppose my very black hair was the giveaway as to my ethnicity. I was the only brunette girl in the group of four girls representing the Rio Grande Valley. Amazingly, it was much ado about nothing! We had no problem at all. No one paid attention to me, so I must have blended in somehow. I managed to pass for a *gringa* because of my light skin. I never told Papá or Mamá of the conversation Mrs. Magueghy had with me. I dread to think how Papá would have reacted!

In Dallas, I learned about the water fountains labels, "Colored only" and "Whites only." What was that all about? I realized what it meant when I saw the African American service workers using the "Colored only" fountain. In the Valley, we did not have any African Americans per se. In all of PSJA High School, we had one African American girl. She had the greatest jovial personality of anyone I have ever known. She made us laugh all the time. Maybe that was her way of coping in an environment so different from her roots. Since Papá worked as a produce buyer, the intermediary, in the agriculture market, he dealt with all the landowners and shippers who were Italian, Jewish, Polish, and Japanese. All these people frequented our home, so I thought nothing of being around other cultures. As I continued to reflect on the issue of prejudice, I was unaware that I would experience the true meaning of prejudice within my own family, personally, later in my life.

I enjoyed being a student, and it seemed to me that many of my classmates knew that I was serious about my studying habits. During homeroom class, which met for just twenty minutes daily, I became friends with David Stoudt and Lewis Smith. David and Lewis were best friends, so having the same homeroom class with both of them was like a treat for all of us. We spent the majority of the class just talking about teachers, classes, and our plans after graduation. Neither David nor Lewis ever seemed concerned about being seen with a Hispanic girl, as some of the *gringo* boys would not even acknowledge my presence at any time or dared to say hello. David and I chatted daily, and he even heard my stories about Papá and his rules. I told him that Papá was like the father referred to in the song "Wolverton Mountain." David did not like school, did only what he had to do to pass a class, and shared with me that he would probably never go to college. He was a very friendly, simple cowboy type, who loved to wear boots to school and did not participate in any sports or organizations.

He became interested in poetry during his senior year, and by the middle of the year, he started playing with words and began writing short poems for fun. Before our graduation, he brought me several poems that he had written to get my opinion on the content. Of course, I was incredibly impressed that he took the time to write and moved by such a personal message given in the lyrics. He told me I could keep them since they were written for me, so I did. I filed them with my high school memorabilia, not realizing what fate had in store for him.

After graduation, he moved to Colorado to work. He was electrocuted accidentally and lived a very short life, only twenty-four years.

To honor his memory, I'm sharing two of his poems in this chapter. I will never forget those days when he read them to me during homeroom class and was so proud of his writing. During an era when boys were to demonstrate their manhood and machismo by showing no emotion, project an image of toughness, and pretend that the stages of life experienced were not to be noted as having the remote possibility of being difficult to accept, David put it in writing. Simply, he was truly a good, kindhearted, and sensitive person, willing to share how he felt through his writing.

During my senior year of high school, I was also elected princess for the homecoming court . . . I sincerely believed that happened only because my sister Teresa, who was a freshman that year, was, and still is, an extreme extrovert. Unlike me, she knew everybody and talked to everybody. She was always very theatrical and beautifully animated. Teresa managed to tell everyone in the freshman class all about my being her older sister. She would even shout it in the school halls as I was passing by. Now, Teresa, that was embarrassing! Every time she did that, I would walk as fast as I could the opposite direction to get away from her and pretend I did not know her. Nevertheless, she got me elected to the homecoming court, so I am grateful to her for being the catalyst that led me to experiencing such a memorable event. The homecoming court presentation during the school day was a memorable one. Papá was out of town during this event, on one of his migratory trips working in Lubbock. Mamá helped me make the dress and prepare for the event. She called her brother in McAllen, Tío Alex, to inform him of the event. He volunteered to be my surrogate father for the event. Tío Alex was very much a gentleman—very polite, courteous, and projected himself as a very cultured man. He escorted me onto the stage, as each one of the princesses needed an escort to present them. The escort would then leave the stage and leave each princess in place for the eventual announcement of the selection of the queen.

One of the candidates, Mary Cano, was escorted to the center of the stage as all other candidates were. As she arrived at the very edge of the stage to make her curtsy, her extremely bouffant petticoat managed to hide the edge of the stage; she slipped off the stage and ever so gracefully, as if floating in a cloud of petticoat netting, landed in the open area before the first row of seats in the auditorium. The audience reacted with a very concerned sigh of *ahh*! Tío Alex was there in a split second, lifting her up off the floor and carrying her off to the side to see if she was hurt. She was not seriously hurt, just a sprained ankle. Tío was the talk of the school for days. The school paper credited Tío for being quite a gentleman in responding to the need so promptly. What chivalrous behavior! I was now even gleaming, telling everyone he was my uncle.

The greatest honor I experienced in high school occurred during the senior awards assembly. The senior faculty chose to award me the Danforth Foundation Award in recognition of leadership qualities. To have teachers recognize my leadership qualities was really an honor when I was not even a cheerleader or in any athletic team, let alone aware that the teachers were observing my leadership skills. I was thrilled that adults chose to recognize me.

I fell in love for the first time during my senior year in high school. Rey was a great student, and I met him through my English IV class. He was smart, nice, quiet, and very much a gentleman. I looked forward to going to class daily just to see him, like a young girl experiencing a "Young Love" for the very first time. He came from a family of super-high achievers. His oldest brothers were all very good students as was he. He was the valedictorian of our senior class and decided to go to the University of Texas in Austin upon completion of high school. We never dated or saw each other outside of the school grounds. Since he was also Catholic, we would visit at church functions. We did not even go to the prom our senior year. Papa's rules were in place, and I knew better than to even try asking for permission to go. Rey understood the rules because his parents were as strict with his sisters as Papá was with me. Rey went on to UT, and I stayed at home, using the summer to plan my entrance to Pan American College in Edinburgh, just an eight-mile commute from home. This was the beginning of what changed the course of the rest of my life. Rey and I continued to communicate by mail during the fall semester of 1962.

When graduation day came, I was a wreck emotionally, just realizing that I was not going to have the opportunity to socialize with so many of my classmates on a daily basis, especially Rey, David, Lewis, and many of my Anglo girlfriends that never came to my side of town. They also did not attend our church in the barrio, because if they happened to be Catholic, they attended St. Jude Catholic Church on the other side of the tracks.

Imelda was not able to attend our graduation because a couple of weeks prior to the ceremony, she was hospitalized for an emergency appendectomy. She became very ill when her appendix was on the verge of rupturing, and her whole body became infected just prior to Dr. Long realizing what was happening. Dr. Long performed the surgery, and she was in the hospital for a week and was in no shape to attend the graduation. David and Lewis came to our home to visit her, and I was very surprised that Papá did not tell them to leave. They just stayed about half an hour, and Papá was very courteous and allowed them to visit her in our bedroom. Of course, I was present at all times. But why did Papá allow them to visit when he would not allow any other boys from the barrio or boys that attended church with us to come into our home and visit with us? They were both gringos, fair skinned, and had blue eyes. Was it because they looked European and not dark skinned like most of the barrio people amongst us?

Since I was going to be home all summer after my high school graduation, without having much to do other than housework, I asked Papá if I could try finding a job for the summer. He said, "What do you want to do?" I responded that I just wanted to have something to do during the day. He agreed that I could apply to work at either a shoe shop or dress shop in McAllen. Again, I was reminded that I was never to work at a restaurant, serving anyone. My brother Loreto drove me to look for a job. I recall driving to McAllen on a Friday and finding a shoe shop on Main Street that was looking for help. I filled out the application while I was in the store and turned it in immediately. The owner of the store, Mr. Vine, immediately interviewed me and hired me on the spot. I was to report to work the next day, Saturday. My job was to stock the shelves daily as soon as I noticed that the shelves were empty. I was also to keep the back room, where all the shoes were, organized by size, color, and inventory number.

More than 90 percent of the customers were from Reynosa, across the U.S. border, so my knowledge of Spanish was an asset. By the middle of the next week, I had memorized the number sequence of the storage room. The job was easy to learn, and I felt comfortable doing it. Mr. Vine observed my work; and at the end of the first week, on a Friday, he called me into his office to talk to me. He asked me what my plans were for the fall. I told him my intention was to go to Pan American College in the fall and study education. His response was, "You don't need to go to college. You can continue working here and earn money and before you know it, you will get a raise. You're a fast learner and you can continue to learn this business." I did not answer him. I did not understand why he would not support my going to college. I just said "thank you" and left.

I went home at the end of the day and told Papá and Mamá what Mr. Vine said. Papá in his usual firm, strong demanding tone said, "You are going to college and that SOB is not going to keep you from doing that. You go to work tomorrow and tell him what your plans are and quit the job. He's just another gringo trying to keep you from getting an education and having a better life." I followed Papa's orders and went to work the next day, worked all day, and quitted at the end of the day.

I had a conversation with Mamá about this experience. She explained that many successful people, not of Mexican descent, believed that Mexicans should not be educated. This was a way of keeping the cost of employees down, always paying them only minimum wage or less because that was all they could ever be worth. Another lesson learned on how we were valued.

The Last Mile

As we walk our lonely aisle
Our sigh of sorrow, should be a smile
For tis the time of the year
For being happy and full of cheer.

We have studied through many long seasons
And now we know our many reasons
For doing the things that we have done
And we're not sorry for a single one.

We've known teachers good and bad
Some were happy, some were sad
They tried to teach us, but we didn't try
Now that we're leaving, they could almost cry.

So this is it, our one last thing
This is it for the final fling
The time is here we're in frustration
For this is it, our graduation!

- David Stoudt+

Homecoming Princess Senior year in high school 1961

Pan American College

Know than thyself, presume not God to scan; The proper study of mankind is man.

- Alexander Pope

Attending Pan Am College (now the University of Texas at Pan American) beginning in the fall of 1962 was the beginning of an incredible learning experience about the rest of the world. It was a time to expand from the social and geographic isolation experienced during the elementary and high school years. Pam Am was not a huge college, only about two thousand students, but it certainly was a lot larger than Pharr-San Juan-Alamo High School. It was a commuter college where the majority of the students were Hispanics, and many of the professors were teachers who had retired in other states and came to South Texas to earn a second income. The student population also consisted of many foreign students from all over the world. Many students were from Central American countries. I met students from Mexico, Lebanon, Panama, Argentina, Chile, and Brazil. The basketball team was an exciting part of campus life. It was the talk of the college because we had players that were very competitive and known nationally for their incredible athletic talents and skills. Going to basketball games was a priority set by many students.

At the age of seventeen, I started college, carrying fifteen semester hours. I studied the course-selection guide meticulously, reading every instruction in the huge leaflet printed every semester. I knew I wanted to be a teacher and major in home economics, so my plan was set. Majoring in home economics and English as a minor was the goal.

My first year—filled with a wealth of learning about systems, schedules, carpooling, finances, people's social interactions, clubs, and professors—was an eye-opening, and many times an overwhelming, experience. A major, early learning experience dealt with what the systems' expectations were of a Hispanic student. This was evident when I met with a counselor prior to registration, and I was advised to sign up for a remedial English 113x class. Why? Because the stigma that came with a Hispanic surname was that I had not learned the English language correctly; therefore, I belonged in a remedial class. I had had a great year as an English IV student in high school. Ms. Brooks, my English IV teacher in high school, even recognized me for the excellent work I did on my research paper on Charles Dickens. Questioning authority was not an option. I did as the advisor recommended and registered for the remedial English class. I suppose that was the profiling of the era!

On the first day of English class, we were given an assignment to write a three-paragraph essay. I do not remember what I wrote on; but on our second class meeting, the professor, Dr. Harwell, asked to see me after class. I was terrified! What did I do wrong? (It was the Irish nuns' guilt teaching at work.) He wanted to know why I had registered to be in that class level. I told him the advisor recommended it. He informed me I was assigned to the wrong class and that I demonstrated skills that belonged in an advanced English class. He happened to be teaching the advanced level also, so he recommended I change to his advanced class. I had to present a form signed by him to have my schedule changed. I did as he recommended immediately. As time went on, Dr. Harwell became my mentor and advisor. Typical of most college plans, I changed the plan midway through my college career. The home economics program was forced to close due to lack of interest from the student population. Consequently, I changed my major areas of study to English and Spanish and managed to get enough hours in home economics to get a minor in it.

Spanish was an easy choice since I had been bilingual all my life, and I barely hit the books taking two levels of Spanish in high school. I must have enjoyed being a student of English because I would stay up every weeknight until two or three in the morning, reading the original works assigned in the classes. Undertaking English as a major was quite a challenge. I relied on *Webster's Unabridged Dictionary* daily to get me through my readings . . . especially the original English writings. I never started studying until after ten in the evening because before that time there were too many duties to cover at home. It was also difficult to concentrate with all of my brothers and sisters moving around and the TV on. Therefore, I created my own schedule and stayed up while everybody else was asleep. Papá would wake up about one in the morning to walk to the bathroom and always made the same comment, "Todavía estas aquí muchacha!" (You're still here, girl!) "Si Papá, todavía no acabo" (Yes, Papa, I am still not finished). I studied every day, never taking for granted that I could wing any class, even my Spanish classes. I also enjoyed spending every opportunity I had in the college library. I loved the quiet solitude and relaxing atmosphere, and I could never get enough of it. For me, it was a place to retreat to and get away from all of the responsibilities I had at home, cooking daily, doing dishes, ironing, and helping with my younger siblings. I could clear my mind and fill it with information that my brain was eager to store.

Socially, I met many different girls from all over the Valley. The Commons was the area of the college grounds where we all met and talked. We hung out there between classes and sometimes even studied there instead of the library. It was common knowledge that if you wanted to meet new people, or find out who was who, just hang out at the Commons. I remember seeing Juan for the first time at the Commons. Needless to mention, he attracted attention because of his height (not too many six-foot Hispanics around during that era), strong masculine features, dark skin, and being dressed very businesslike daily (white shirt, dark slacks, with black-rimmed glasses)—definitely tall, dark, and handsome! He even wore bow ties to class. I had never seen anyone wear bow ties daily! I did not speak to him at all for a very long time. I just watched. One of my many distant cousins Ana Maria Fernandez, who lived in Edinburg, was also at Pan Am, and she knew Juan from having had classes with him in previous years. I used to visit with her regularly at the Commons, and one day she said that Juan wanted to know why I would not speak to him when he would approach me and tried to start a conversation. My response: "No one had ever introduced me to him, and I did not speak to any boys unless I was properly introduced." She related my response to him, and his answer very simply was, "Well, introduce me." He later claimed to me that he seriously believed that my nose was so high up in the air, that nobody could possibly reach it. I suppose he was not used to formalities.

The following day, early in October of 1962, Ana Maria introduced us properly, and Juan started coming into the Commons almost daily to sit and talk with me. He did most of the talking. He was quite a conversationalist. He was president of the Neumann Club, member of the Intercollegiate Knights, worked part-time since he was ten years old, and told all kinds of stories about his behavior while growing up and attending junior high school and high school in Raymondville. He would brag about how he knew the principal of the junior high very well, frequenting his office on a regular basis! I definitely concluded that it was not because of academic issues, but certainly because of his behavior in the classroom. His eyes beamed with pride every time he addressed his familiarity with the principal's office.

Juan always had something to say and asked many, many questions.

"Where are you from?"

"Where do you live?"

"Do you have a boyfriend?" When I responded yes, another question followed:

"Where is he?"

"He's attending the University of Texas at Austin," I would answer with great pride.

His comment: "That is not good, porque amor de lejos, es amor de pendejo" (a faraway love is an idiot's love).

Every time he saw me, he asked the same question about the Austin boyfriend. As time went on, the circle of male and female friends all knew that I had a boyfriend in Austin. They also knew that I never saw him, but that we wrote each other almost daily, and that I would probably see him only during the holidays when he would come home to Pharr to visit with his family. Everyone was aware of Papa's rules because that was just part of the culture, even though many of my friends' parents would let go of many of the dating rules by the time the girls were out of high school. Papá never did!

During that first semester, I also met another young man who was very nice, respectful, and very handsome. He was of Spanish decent and came from a family who was connected with the community politically. His style of interaction with me was very different. He would have his very loyal friends (Joe "Rosie" Longoría, a huge hefty-looking guy, and Chore, a very small person no more than three feet tall, who was loved by everyone who met him) visit with me daily and find out what was going on with my life. It was very surprising to me that I was getting so much attention! I certainly was not used to that! Besides, I was not allowed to date, so how could I possibly develop relationships with boyfriends within the college scene? Besides, I had a boyfriend! My focus remained with my studies.

Rey and I continued our letter writing as I did a lot of thinking as to where our future would lead us. He came home for Thanksgiving, and I saw him at a church function. He was becoming very impatient about not being allowed to go out on dates with me. He wanted me to just approach Papá and ask him to let me go out with him when he came home. I knew that was not possible. Papá would never go for it. So he went back to UT disappointed with my lack of initiative in addressing his request, and the letter-writing routine continued as usual until I received a letter from him a couple of weeks before Christmas in 1962 where he stated "when we get married." When we what?

Wait a minute, what did he mean "when we get married"? I was never asked! He just assumed that I was going to marry him because we were going together. I don't think so! I thought about it for a day and decided to write him a "Dear John letter" immediately. I was only eighteen, naïve and sheltered about many things in life, but I knew that I was the one who was going to make the decision as to whom I was going to marry. Not my parents, not my siblings, not even the boyfriend whom I sincerely cared for was going to make a lifetime decision for me without asking me, when I was not even ready to make it on my own. I don't know if, after reading his letter, I was shocked at the realization that I felt I was being taken for granted or that I was perceived as not being able to decide for myself what I wanted in life. Whatever the reason, I wrote the letter and mailed it. I remember specifically asking him not to write me again. I felt I needed the freedom to think for myself. Being the gentleman that he was, he complied with my request.

I continued going to college in the spring semester of 1963, and in no time word was out that I no longer had a boyfriend. The very good-looking Spaniard from Edinburg, Tavo, began to look for me daily and managed to get his friends to walk me to classes all the time. The feedback from his friends was always very complimentary, always reminding me that he was very interested in me and that he wanted to date me and be my formal boyfriend. All the month of January I heard this, so by the first week in February I decided to start visiting with him in college and met him for lunch and soda breaks. He was quite a gentleman, supposedly very much in love with me. He protected me as if I were a prized jewel. He literally treated me like a china doll. All this was new to me as far as a boy-girl relationship was concerned. He treated me with so much respect I thought surely he deserved my attention.

As I continued visiting with my Edinburg girlfriends (one happened to be Tavo's cousin), I learned that he had had a girlfriend since he was in junior high school. Supposedly, his family did not approve of the girl because she came from a single-mother home with very little rules. This was not common in the Hispanic community during the sixties. She was free to go out with him at any time and dressed showing a lot of skin, both actions forbidden in my household and by his family.

I continued trying to develop a relationship with him during the month of February, but as I tried, I discovered more and more about his relationship with the junior high girlfriend. Actually, he never stopped seeing her during the time that he started courting me. She began calling me at home and leaving messages about her never letting him go. At first, I just listened and would mention to Tavo her phone calls whenever I saw him. It is a good thing Mamá would answer the phone most of the time or else I would have had a lot of explaining to do if Papá had answered.

"Who is she? Who are her parents? Does she go to college? Is she Catholic?"

She was not in college nor was she Catholic . . . AND coming from a single-parent home in a divorce situation . . . I would have had a lot of explaining to do, picking those kinds of friends to call me at home. Another of Papa's constant reminders was always in the recesses of my mind: "Dime con quien andas y te dire quien eres" (You can judge a man by the company he keeps).

Tavo always said she meant nothing to him and for me to ignore her blabbing. Well I tried until Rodeo Days celebration came to campus during the latter part of February. Tavo wanted me to go to the Rodeo with him, but I knew Papá would not let me go, so I did not even bother to ask. I told Tavo I would not be allowed to go. The day after he asked me to go to the Rodeo, his girlfriend called me at home and told me that she knew I was not allowed to date and that she was, so she was going with him regardless of what my relationship was with him. She was going to have him because she could give him whatever he wanted. At that moment, without thinking or hesitation, I told her she could have him. I was not going to be a part of this type of games, nor was I going to compete with anyone for his affection. I informed her that I would inform him of my decision immediately. I hung up and immediately called Tavo. I told him about my conversation with his other girlfriend and that I was not going to be a part of any games. I also informed him that the next day I was returning all the gifts he had given me—two rings and his picture. He was to return my picture also . . . my picture was already being displayed in the family living room because he had informed his mother, a widow, that I was the girl he was going to marry. The next morning, all items in hand, I met him by one of the sidewalks on campus and returned all the items. I never spoke a word. I just handed him the items and walked away. For several months after that, Rosie and Chore encouraged me to get back with Tavo because his other girlfriend meant nothing to him. I was naïve, but not that naïve! In addition, I was very much aware of some cultural norms like married men who found it quite acceptable to not only have a wife but also a mistress. That was not my idea of a successful future relationship in a marriage. That was the end of that. I was very disappointed in myself, realizing that I actually believed what Tavo led me to believe. I suppose "Everybody's Somebody's Fool" at least once in our lives. That was definitely me being very gullible.

Spring on campus was full with all kinds of activities, parades, banquets, and formal dances. The Bougainvillea Ball was a big deal on campus. A very formal dance with a live orchestra playing the ballroom-dancing type music was the ultimate of a social event. Never in my wildest dreams did I ever imagine that I would be asked to go to such a function. Lo and behold, a couple of weeks before the dance, Juan approaches me and asks if I would go with him to the ball.

My response was that I would have to ask Papá permission, and I would let him know in a few days. What in the world possessed me to respond with such hope? I was so surprised by his request that I decided to take a chance and ask Papá if I could go. Of course, I spoke to Mamá about it first, and she advised me to ask him and find out what he would say. Of course, he said no immediately, and the interrogation began: "Who was this Juan guy? Who does he think he is wanting to take you out? Does he think that every Tom, Dick, and Harry can come into this house and take you anywhere?" I just said he was a young man I met in college, and he wanted to take me to the ball. Papá said no.

Mamá recommended I wait a couple of days for Papá to get over the initial shock of me wanting to have a date and for him to cool down and think about it. Papá talked to my brother Loreto Jr. (Lee), a year younger than me, and asked him about Juan. Lee, of course, said that he was a nice guy studying business accounting who just wanted to take me to a dance. A couple of days later, Papá called me to his room (my stomach was now churning with butterflies all over, which was the usual feeling I felt every time Papá called me to his room for a lecture or interrogation) and told me I could go to the ball. Lee was to drive me to the dance, and we were to return by 10:30 p.m. I walked out of Papa's room ecstatic. Wow, I cannot believe it! He said yes. What would I wear? Mamá had helped me make the dress that I wore a year ago for the homecoming court, and I could still wear that one with some minor adjustments. Lee told Papá he would take care of me, and of course the rule was that we were not to be alone. Lee assured Papá he would follow the rules.

The night came for the dance, and Lee drove me to the ball. Lee informed me that he was going to visit with a Panamanian exchange student whom he had a crush on. I did not have a clue what to expect, so I was fine with Lee's plan. Juan was waiting for me at the parking lot of the ballroom. He borrowed a friend's car to go to the dance because he did not own a car. He looked sharp dressed in "A White Sport Coat (and a Pink Carnation)" and greeted me with a beautiful pink wrist corsage. I was in my pink formal gown with lots of ruffles and lace and petticoats. Need I mention, when Lee dropped me off, he told me he would come back to pick me up later. Lee did not stick around at all. I assumed he would pick me up by 10:00 p.m. so that we would be home as Papá dictated.

Yes, I felt like Cinderella! The dance was great! A live band played big band sounds plus many Latin sounds. Wow, could Juan dance! AND he was such a gentleman, exhibiting all the courtesies (pulling my chair every time I moved, leading me to the dance floor holding my hand, bringing me the punch to drink, never leaving me alone) I expected of a gentleman. He informed me that he had taken ballroom dancing and enjoyed dancing. All I did was follow. Yes, he could dance—polka, Paso Doble, rock and roll, boogie, slow dancing, you name it, and he could do it. IN ADDITION, he loved showing off his steps. Juan knew everybody! He introduced me to so many people, I did not have a clue who they were or how he knew them. We danced every single tune the band played. Time flew! Lee shows up around 10:45 p.m. and begins visiting with several people. We had already broken curfew! Juan walked me out, and I was already a nervous wreck, worried about what Papá would say or do when we got home. I thanked Juan for the great evening and went home. I probably fell in love with him that evening. We got home after eleven, and everyone was asleep except Mamá. I tiptoed into the house through the back door, and Mamá met me to ask me how it went. Of course, I told her all about Juan's dancing skills and that it was a great evening. She was happy and pleased for me. Next morning, Papá reprimanded me for not getting home on time. My only comment on that was that Lee was a little late leaving the dance because he was talking with all his friends. Lee discussed with Papá that he lost track of time talking with people. Subject closed. Another cultural norm: a man's word (especially the firstborn son's) is always more valuable than any woman's.

Come Monday morning back on campus, I found out from the daily Commons visitors late in the day that the guys were calling Juan "Cinderella" because I left the dance before midnight. His friends, especially Beto Esquivel, his best friend, gave him a hard time and wanted to know if I was going to turn into a pumpkin if I did not get home by midnight. Juan had returned to the dance when I left, so all his friends started asking him what happened to me. He just told them that I had a curfew and had to be home early. That night, Juan swore to all his friends he would never ask me out again because Papá was too strict, and it was impossible to live by his rules. I seriously reflected on that comment, and I did not blame him a bit for deciding that. When I saw him later in the day, he did thank me for going with him and said he enjoyed it. He, personally, never told me that he would not ask me out again.

Tavo's friends who knew about Papa's rules also gave me a hard time. How had I managed to go to a dance with Juan? There were comments like, "*Primita* (little cousin, a term of endearment used to address anyone you would like to be part of your family), we thought your Papá was too strict to let you go anywhere."

"Papa is still strict, but my brother drove me and was with me most of the time." Somehow, that response was acceptable, and discussion closed on that topic.

I continued to see Juan on campus, and we would chat, but only about classes and professors. Since we only had a few more weeks before the end of the semester, I had to hit the books as usual and prepare for finals. I remained focused, trying to reach my objectives. Before the end of the semester, Beto informed me that Juan was now interested in a very tall, slim girl, and he had asked her out. I concluded he was no longer interested in pursuing any relationship with me.

The summer came, and I enrolled in summer school. On a usual visit at the Commons at the end of June, Juan sits and chats about taking a semester off and joining the army reserve. He had been attending college on loans and needed money, so he saw the military as a way to earn some income and be able to come back after a six-month basic training and resume his studies. After the initial six-month training, he would have to do weekend duty on a monthly basis.

My usual, I just listened and said nothing. I knew he did not have any financial resources, so I realized this was a good option for him. At the beginning of July, he and Beto joined the Army National Guard and went to basic training at Fort Polk Louisiana, an army base near Leesville, Louisiana. The future annual two-week summer training was to be held at Fort Hood near Killeen, Texas. The six-month basic training being scheduled to end at the end of December was perfect timing for both of them to return to begin the spring college semester. Of course, since the Viet Nam war was in full force, there would always be a possibility that the reserves would be called to serve.

One of the courses I took that summer was chemistry. I was required to take the course if I wanted to be certified to teach home economics. To my surprise, I thoroughly enjoyed studying the content of the course, and I especially enjoyed the lab work. I could see a relationship between the lab experiments and cooking. There were only three girls—Betty, Jane, and me—in the class. Betty was taking the course in hopes of studying pharmacy in the future. Jane and I were there because of our interest in home economics.

Our professor, Mr. Chauvinist, told the class one day that chemistry was a very difficult course, and women did not belong in his class. He informed the class that he did not believe we, the girls in class, were capable of learning the material and that we were a hazard to the other students when doing our chemistry experiments. After hearing him make those statements, I decided I was going to study harder than ever and prove him wrong. All three of us survived the class and managed never to blow up the lab.

I continued with my summer studies, and before I knew it, it was time for the fall semester to begin. As I was registering for my classes, I was asked to go to the financial area for information. I did not know what that meant because I always paid for my classes with a check from Papá. He would just sign a check and let me fill in whatever amount the tuition was. I would later get the money to buy the books needed for each class. I was thrilled to discover the education department awarded me a scholarship. I tucked away Papa's check and went home ecstatic about my news. Mamá was very proud of me, but not Papá. He believed that it was an insult to his manhood to accept charity, as he referred to the scholarship. He went on and on about how he did not need strangers paying for his children's education. He believed that was his responsibility and no one else's. Mamá and I tried to explain to him the difference between a scholarship and charity, but for some reason he never accepted our explanation. I thought a lot about Papa's reaction. I came to the realization that his belief is that the man of the house, and only the man of the house, should be the sole provider and responsible for the future of his children's education. He had never allowed our mother to go back to work because he passionately believed that meant he could not provide for his own family, and what would people in the community think of him. The image that the man of the house should project to the community is that he can provide for every need the family has. Evidently, the power of pride and exhibiting it was far more important than facing the reality that educating a large family with Papa's earning abilities was eventually going to become an impossible goal to reach.

I did not hear a word about Juan for at least two months. Beto came back to Edinburgh for a family-emergency visit, and I came across him in the library. His father was very ill in his deathbed, and he was actually looking for Peggy, a close friend of mine. He had a serious crush on her. He questioned me about why I had not written Juan. My answer was that I had no idea he expected me to write, nor did he ever share his address with me. He said that Juan had tried writing the girl he had dated before he left, but she did not answer. He always made a joke of any rejections they experienced with girlfriends. In this case, a Mexican song by Pedro Infante alludes to a man being in love with Eufemia, who writes her a letter to tell her so, and she never responds. Beto's comment was, "No contestó Eufemia" (Eufemia did not answer). I gave Beto my address, which I knew Juan already had because he knew where I lived, and informed him that if I received a letter, I would respond.

Beto must have returned with the message, because within a week, I received a letter from Juan, telling me all about his experience in the military. I answered every letter. He continued writing me when he could. His schedule was gruesome, many days with very little time left for letter writing. We continued our friendly letter communication until the end of the semester. He never gave me exact return dates. He did not have a telephone in his home in Raymondville, so if he wanted to call me, he had to use a public phone. He called once from Ft. Polk, a pleasant surprise since he was a penny pincher and would repeatedly share with me he never had money. A godsend was that he picked to call me at home during a time when Papá was not home to answer the phone. Otherwise, I would not have had the opportunity to chat with him. Papá always hung up the phone as soon as he realized the party on the other side was the voice of a male asking to speak to any of his daughters.

I continued my heavy college load, carrying twenty-one hours of course work, leaving no time for anything else other than studies. Dr. Dominquez, one of my advanced Spanish professors, offered me a part-time job translating documents from Spanish to English. I was paid $1.25 an hour, the federal minimum wage for 1963, for every hour I spent translating documents, mostly minutes, from the Organization of American States that Dr. Dominguez belonged to and had an officer's position. It was great to earn a few additional dollars on my own so I would not have to ask Papá for money every week for my carpool expenses and bus expenses. It was also beneficial to me to practice the translation process as now I was majoring in English and Spanish. I carpooled with Melba, the owner of the two-door green Plymouth car, along with three other girls all from Pharr. Each one of us contributed a dollar a week for the carpool, and with the four dollars collected from her passengers, Melba would fill up the car for the week and had money left over. We were always on the lookout for 19 cents a gallon gasoline, any brand, any station. We always managed to find one weekly. This method of transportation was also far more economical than riding the VTC bus daily to campus, as that cost 70¢ round-trip daily. I saved $10 a month by riding the carpool instead of the bus.

On a Friday, as I had finished attending a Spanish class, I was walking to meet my carpool at the parking lot when I came across Rosie, Joe Longoria, and he asked me loudly, "Have you heard?"

"Have I heard what?" I asked.

"President Kennedy has been assassinated," he said.

"Rosie," I said, "quit joking with me. You shouldn't make up those kinds of jokes."

"I'm not joking, primita. It's true, it just happened. Listen to the radio on the way home and you'll find out its true."

I turned around to observe the other students around me and realized everybody was talking about the same thing. Oh my God! It was true! All five of us girls in the carpool got in the car and listened to the radio all the way home. We were numb! That weekend the TV was on all the time, and our home was very quiet with a melancholy air about it. We all cried freely, watching all the events covered on TV.

About mid-December, I was standing by the card catalog in the library, reviewing information for my last exams for the semester, when a tall figure stood behind me. I turned once and thought I do not know who it is, so I ignored him. He gets closer and says, "How are you doing?" I turned again to see who was talking, and to my surprise, it was Juan with his usual wide smile. He was so thin, I did not recognize him. He had lost at least fifty pounds and had the GI haircut. Except for his contagious smile, he looked very different. We chatted awhile about why he was on campus. He was looking for information to register for the spring semester and was negotiating his living accommodations while attending college. He rented a room with the Rodriguez family in Edinburgh. He did not have any transportation yet, so he borrowed his dad's pickup to take care of business for the next semester. He walked to all his classes; for social activities, his friends would lend him a car or pick him up for the event. He also got a part-time job as a junior accountant with a CPA firm for the spring semester. He had things in order for returning to his studies. I had to study for my finals, so the conversation was short. I thought he looked great!

The next semester glared me in the face with the usual twenty-one hours of course work. Now I was determined to get my degree in a three-year period, and I was already halfway there. Papá was already paying for three of us to go college, and if I did not finish in three years, he would have to pay for four of us in college at the same time. We all commuted, so he was not concerned with dorm fees, but keeping a family with eleven children going was not easy financially. I continued focusing on my classes. I saw Juan in the Commons occasionally. With his unique sense of humor, he would offer to buy me a Coke and finish the offering with, "You better hurry up and make up your mind, I only have one quarter left and the next girl that walks by will get the offer if you say no." I always accepted with laughter. I had met two of his cousins Maria Alicia Garza and Elma Campos from Los Saenz, the city where he was born. They would hang out with me in the Commons and many times enjoyed commenting on Juan's way of trying to impress me, offering to buy me a drink. What an attention-getting approach. He got a lot of laughter from all of us; that approach never stopped.

I continued to meet other students on campus. Basketball season was in full swing and a very popular social activity to attend. The Broncos had won the National Association of Intercollegiate Athletics national championship the year before, so basketball games had standing-room-only crowds. Juan never asked me out after he returned, so I concluded friends were all we would continue to be.

A young man I met from San Benito, Ruben, asked me if I would like to go to the basketball game. I explained to him about Papa's rules. He understood and agreed that I could meet him there. I was not seriously interested, but he seemed very nice and courteous, so I said yes. As usual, my brother would drive me to the game. Out of nowhere, Juan calls me at home a couple of days before the game. He wanted to know if I was going to the game Friday evening. I said I was not sure yet. It depended on whether my brother could borrow Papa's car. That part was true. Since I was not going, he tells me then he was not going either. I took a deep breath and said, "Thank you, God."

My brother Lee did get to borrow Papa's car, so we made our plans to go. I met Ruben at the entrance of the gym and went in to sit about midway up the bleachers. The games were always exciting and enjoyable. I was very involved in the game at the beginning of the second quarter when I glanced toward the double-door entrance to the gym, and my heart stopped. There was Juan coming in by himself. He stood there just eyeing the stands. Dear Lord! Please don't let him see me! I pretended not to see him. Before I knew it, he was approaching the same bleacher we had picked. He stands in front of me, greets me with a jovial "hi, how are you doing?" and sits himself down between Ruben and me. Ruben moved over and never said a word. I was dumbfounded. I just stared, trying to figure out what just happened. This is not happening! Juan chatted about how he thought he was not going to make the game but found a ride the last minute. He sat there for at least fifteen minutes. It seemed like a lifetime. Just as smoothly as he seated himself between Ruben and me, he got up, said good-bye, and left. I was numb! Why would he do such a thing? Nothing I could say or do could mend this very awkward incident. The game was finally over. Ruben and I went our separate ways. Need I mention, Ruben never asked me out again? If Juan had a hidden goal to keep this very nice young man from asking me out again, he accomplished it that evening!

The next time I saw Juan on campus, his grin was so wide I could not help but just laugh with him. "I thought you weren't going to the game," he said.

"I wasn't. Lee got Papa's car the last minute and we decided to go," I said.

"OK," he said. "Before we decide to go to any more games, let's talk to each other ahead of time." I agreed.

The basketball-game event must have gotten his attention because every time he would see me on campus he wanted to know if I was going anywhere during the week. Of course I was. The library was where I spent every waking minute if I was not in a classroom. So he could find me there almost every day. The library had several small study rooms with large tables, and I always tried to locate one and spread out all my books and papers for my study time. That semester, we met a lot in the library and did a lot of conversing about personal plans. He now planned to finish his business degree by May of 1965, and I hoped to finish by August of 1965. One day he walked me to my advanced Spanish class and bids me farewell with, "Ay te watcho!"

"Ay te what?" was my response! What does "watcho" mean?

"You know, from 'watch' with your eyes," was his response, grinning as usual. Wow, was I in for another learning experience about the use of language. That was a neologism! I was going into a formal advanced Spanish language class, and here I am listening to what I learned later was to become known as Tex-Mex. I never heard that kind of Spanish in our home. We spoke only the formal Spanish. I suppose maybe because my Spanish grandparents only spoke the formal language and no English.

He decided to ask me if I would go with him to a formal dinner dance in early May 1965. Papá was out of town, so I asked Mamá, and she said that was fine. She knew of Juan's family because she was familiar with the family names from the Roma-Los Sáenz area. She would just mention that the Morenos she knew about from Los Saenz were good, hardworking, and respectable people.

By now, I had discussed with our pastor, Fr. Donald Haile, OMI, about Juan. Fr. Haile was a very caring priest who kept track of many families in his parish. I was the church organist and translated the sermons he wrote from English to Spanish. He was fluent in Spanish but felt he needed help with the formal delivery of a homily. He did very well for a New York Irishman who had never spoken Spanish before in his life until he began his studies as an oblate priest. I did not receive any monetary compensation for any of these services. It was just part of my volunteer work at church, and it was great practice for my advanced Spanish classes.

There were several times when I was followed all the way home from the college campus. I rode the bus home many times when carpools could not be worked out. Boys who had cars and wanted to know where I lived would follow me all the way to Pharr, seven miles away. Usually, the follower would be a boy I had just met, and I would not divulge much information about myself. I was scared of what could happen if any boy grabbed me when I was by myself. Since many families did not allow their girls to date, it was common practice for would-be suitors to drive by the homes of the girls they were interested in courting. Juan's comments on this practice was that the boys, in an effort to impress the girls, would cruise in their old cars with all the windows rolled up, pretending they had an air-conditioned car when in reality they were suffocating from the heat generated inside the car without air-conditioning. Nevertheless, it was a good attempt to impress the girls! I was always careful and watched to see if anyone was following me.

When I noticed someone was following the bus, I would get off at the usual bus stop at the corner of Hwy 281 and West Hawk Street and go directly to the church office, just half a block away from the bus drop-off. The church secretary was always there, so I knew someone would answer the door. I would inform Fr. Haile what was going on, and I would stay in his office chatting about college activities and classes. He was very aware of all the cultural norms, so when I mentioned I had met Juan, he asked about how I was going to handle any dating. I informed him about Juan's request to go to a formal dinner dance with him, and since Papá was out of town on business, Mamá had given me permission to go. He always asked to keep him updated. After about half an hour of catching him up on my schedule, he would walk home with me, just a half block away. By then, the admirer, tired of driving around the block several times, was gone.

My sister Teresa babysat regularly for one of her high school teachers. Again, her extrovert personality came into play for this event. She mentioned to Mrs. Williams that I was going to a formal ball and that I was all excited about it. Mrs. Williams offered to lend me any part of her wardrobe that I needed for the event. She brought over to our home several dresses for me to look at and see if I liked any of them. A two-piece full-length gown with a mandarin collar jacket fit me perfectly. It was made of a burgundy and gold brocade material. I could have sworn some tailor had fitted me for it. It was perfect! I decided I would wear that to the ball and thanked Mrs. Williams endlessly for sharing her wardrobe.

Since Papá was not home, Mamá allowed Juan to pick me up at the house. He borrowed a friend's car to go to the dance and picked me up early in the evening by 6:00 p.m. Fr. Haile came over to the house before six to see how things were going. I figured out later that he probably just wanted to know what I was wearing and see if it was appropriate for a date. I passed the visual test. Dinner began at six thirty, so Juan came to the door precisely at 6:00 p.m., carrying a see-through plastic box with a wrist corsage with an orchid surrounded by white carnations. He was dressed in a dark brown suit, brown tie, and a maroon buttoner that matched my dress. We were set to go. Mamá just told us to be careful and to be back before midnight. What a thrill! My first real date at the age of twenty only because Papá was gone, and Mamá allowed it!

Again, the dance was with a live band. This time the music was not as fast as the previous dance I had attended with Juan. That was a good thing! My dress was not made to polka! It turned out to be an evening full of hormone awakening. Juan held me all the time. He could not keep his hands off me. We danced all the slow dances: "Strangers in the Night," "Spanish Eyes," "Smoke Gets in Your Eyes," "Donna," and "16 Candles." This was it! I was immersed in a fairy-tale story that I never wanted to end. On our way home at the end of the evening, we had a great conversation about how enjoyable the evening was. Before getting

96 Carmen Treviño Moreno

out of the car, he held me and kissed me with such tenderness, yet with a strong sense of confidence, that it seemed so natural and right for me to let him do it. Every hormone in my body took a live form and awakened like flowers bursting into bloom at the onset of spring! I had never felt like this "'Til I Kissed You." I was on cloud nine by the time I got into the house.

Mamá waited up for me and asked how things went. I just answered that it was fine and that I had a great time. She was happy for me. Papá came home from his trip a couple of weeks later, and Mamá never mentioned to him that I had a date. I was glad that stayed between us.

Juan at Fort Polk, Louisiana in 1963

Juan and I in May 1965

Lifelong Decisions

To accomplish great things, we must not only act, but also dream;
not only plan, but also believe.

- Anatole France

It was now time for Juan to get ready for his graduation, which was coming up at the end of May. Both he and I were immersed in our studies for our final exams. We met in the library every opportunity we had, and on Saturday mornings after my three-hour class, we met at the local Pierce Café just a block from the college. Rocky, a short and stocky-built special-needs adult, was always our waiter. He memorized our standard order, a doughnut a la mode and a Coke. That's all Juan could afford. We spend at least an hour every Saturday morning talking about classes, family, and future prospects for jobs. The first thing he did prior to his graduation was buy a '55 Ford for $300. Now he had transportation to move to Brownsville and begin working for the CPA firm that had hired him as soon as he graduated. He rented a garage apartment in downtown Brownsville on Elizabeth Street. He furnished it with used furniture.

About a week before his graduation, we had a very serious conversation about our feelings toward each other. He shared that he sincerely believed he loved me and wanted me to be in his life forever. He also shared that his father always told him not to confuse true love with the feeling of just wanting to go to bed with a woman. Love is much more than that. Wow! This is what I wanted to hear. To seriously ponder and consider living the rest of your life with someone is no easy decision, and it requires a major commitment up front. That day I decided he was the one I wanted to marry someday.

A week prior to his graduation day, he asked if I would attend the graduation ceremony. I said I'd have to figure out a way to get there because Papá would probably not let me go. My best friend, Peggy, from Hidalgo, knew all about Papá and his rules, and she was always very attentive, listening to my ordeal dealing with Papa's rules. Both Peggy and I started college at the same time. We both majored in English and minored in Spanish, and we were both involved in the Catholic Newman Club in college. We took many classes together and had the same circle of friends on the college campus. We also both decided to finish college in three years, so our commonalities were many.

Peggy suggested I tell Papá that I wanted to go to the graduation ceremony with her and her mom because they invited me to join them. Peggy actually was going because Beto was also graduating, and they had been dating for a while. Her mom was the postmaster in Hidalgo, and Papá accepted that having her as a chaperone would suffice. I asked Papá if I could go to the ceremony with Mrs. Wilkison and Peggy. Of course, I did not say it was because Juan was graduating. I just said they had invited me to go. He said yes. Mrs. Wilkison and Peggy picked me up at home, and I went to the ceremony with them. I was so glad I had them; otherwise, I would not have attended Juan's graduation.

After the graduation ceremony, I met Juan, hugged him, and congratulated him. He introduced me to his parents, a very different couple compared to my parents. His father was very short in stature; and his mother, with very strong features, had a larger body frame than his father. I, embarrassed, merely extended my hand and said, "Mucho gusto." Juan wanted us to go out for dinner with him, but Mrs. Wilkison told him they had to get me home soon or Papá would be upset. That was the end of our celebration.

The following day, Juan called me at home and very firmly wanted to know if I had made a definite commitment to marrying him. This was the second time he asked. He wanted an answer so he could move on with life and begin planning. I had already decided I did want to marry him but constantly worried about Papá and his rules and expectations. That day I decided I would marry him, but how was I going to deal with Papá and all of his rules? I again said I was thinking about it but that I wanted to get my degree first before making any commitments.

He wanted to get married immediately after my graduation. That was not going to happen. "I need a year to work and time to figure out how to ask Papá for permission to get married," I said. I was not going to elope, run away, or do anything that was not acceptable with my parents or against church rules. He agreed to let me think about how we could plan this and let him know after my graduation in three months.

Less than a month later, his brother George was getting married in McAllen, and my cousin Julia Del Rosario Fierros was asked to sing at the wedding. On occasion, I accompanied her as her organist at several weddings, especially during the summer months. This was a welcomed opportunity as it meant that I would be paid anywhere from ten to fifteen dollars for each wedding. Julia had an operatic voice (mezzo-soprano) that made all four walls of any church tremble. The traditional "Bridal Chorus" from *Lohengrin* by Wagner began the wedding procession into the church. Then Julia would sing "The Lord's Prayer" during the Offertory of the Mass; the "Panis Angelicus," by Louis Lambillotte, SJ, also in Latin, during Communion; and Schubert's "Ave Maria" in Latin after Communion, when it was traditional for the bride to present flowers to our Blessed Mother.

Traditionally, brides would seek the guidance and blessing of our Lord, through this symbolic ceremony that requests the intercession of the Blessed Virgin Mary, through prayer and offering of flowers. Mary, the mother of Jesus, is the ultimate role model for the Catholic bride, as she will strive to mirror Mary's perfect love for God and devotion to her family. This part of the marriage ceremony was when the true realization, with tears in their eyes, came to all the mamas present that the young bride was now officially beginning a new life with a new family. The exit piece was always Mendelssohn's "Wedding March."

When Julia called me to arrange for the practices and the wedding, I was not even aware that George was Juan's brother. Juan informed me during a conversation on campus that his brother was getting married to Conchita, a girl from McAllen, and his family heard that I was the organist accompanying the bride's singer friend. I was glad to know that I was now involved in one of Juan's family events. The wedding day came, and all went smoothly with the Mass and the music. After Mass, Juan asked me to join him for the reception, As usual, I had to decline as I did not have permission from Papá to go anywhere except the church and home afterward.

I had a summer full of coursework to do before graduating. I registered for the summer classes, and Papá finally agreed that I could take driving lessons so I could drive to work after graduating. I found a driving teacher from Edinburg that gave private lessons, so both Imelda and I signed up and began to learn to drive. We learned to drive in a car with shift gear that had a clutch. I did not do well at first, but after a couple of weeks, I got the hang of it and managed to pass the course.

Juan worked as a junior accountant with Arturo Flores, CPA, at a firm in Edinburg all summer, so we continued to see each other on campus when he could meet me for a snack on Saturday mornings as had been our custom. I always looked forward to our Saturday morning together. Juan always managed to make me laugh as he had never-ending stories about his adventures living in a poor neighborhood and his survival tricks. He reminded me constantly that a beer-drinking crowd could not live up to a champagne-drinking crowd. Lack of money was always an issue. One of his favorite stories was how he managed to get fresh vegetables for family dinners. The trucks carrying the vegetables that had been picked during the day would drive down his street very slowly at the end of day; and he would run after the truck, jump on it, and touch a few of the vegetables to create a rolling effect. The vegetables are now rolling off the truck into the street, ready to be picked up by the neighborhood kids. I found it amusing that anyone would do that since Papá always brought the vegetables home directly from the fields for us to use.

His stories about his experiences during his six-month boot camp training in Ft. Polk, Louisiana, were revelations. Many of the recruits came from the Appalachia regions, Arkansas, Mississippi, and Louisiana. The majority of these recruits had never seen a vending machine or a public telephone. During one of the company-formation routines, the soldiers were informed by the first sergeant that this group represented the highest level of education they had ever had; a tenth-grade high school education average amongst the 250 recruits. Juan knew at that point that he was definitely returning to college to get a degree.

That same day, the first sergeant informed the recruits that a classification-of-race survey was being taken and for all personnel to fall back as their race was called. The command came: "As I call your race, fall to the rear. All Negroid personnel fall to the rear." All Negroid soldiers obeyed the command. "All Spanish-speaking personnel fall to the rear." Juan did not move. The next command was, "All Caucasian personnel stand fast." Juan stood with the Caucasian group. Now the sergeant repeats the command in a louder tone: "All Spanish-speaking personnel fall to the rear." Juan did not move. The first sergeant again repeated the command for the third time: "ALL Spanish-speaking personnel fall to the rear." Juan did not move. Now the first sergeant addresses Juan, "Moreno, what the hell do you think you are?" "Sir, a Spanish-speaking Caucasian, sir." Then Juan stepped to the rear.

We always discussed the fact that there were only five race categories that humans were categorized as belonging to. Why were we, as Spanish-speaking Caucasians, categorized in a very different category, when in essence, being a Spanish speaker merely meant a culture or ethnicity that we were born into, not a race?

In June, I began filling out applications in the surrounding school districts to see if I could land a job for the fall semester of '65, expecting to get my degree in August of '65. I applied in Pharr, McAllen, and Donna. I got an interview in McAllen ISD. After the superintendent met me, he told me I had no business majoring in secondary education. I was too young to teach in a high school. He said it was unrealistic for me to think I could find a job in any secondary school. He said no one would hire me. I left his office disappointed, discouraged, wondering if he was right. I was only twenty and would not turn twenty-one until the end of September. I suppose that in a high school, I would be teaching students only four or five years younger than me. I refused to give up my search.

I received a call from Donna ISD, informing me that the district needed a language arts teacher for the seventh and eighth grades. Middle school is secondary education, so I agreed to go to the interview. The superintendent interviewed me and immediately sent me to speak to the principal, Mr. Whiteside, at Moye Junior High. He interviewed me and hired me immediately. My assignment was to teach seventh—and eighth-grade language arts and remedial reading. Now I could concentrate on finishing my last twelve hours of coursework to get my degree and certification.

I also had to decide about transportation now that I had a teaching contract. Fr. Haile had a friend who owned a car dealership in Lewisville, Texas, north of Dallas, and he offered to help find me a good deal on a new car. I, of course, thought that was a great avenue to follow. I spoke to Papá about it, and he agreed that it was all right for Fr. Haile to do the research. Fr. Haile made the contact and managed to give me all the information with a brochure and a picture of a four-door '65 Ford Fairlane sedan. The price of $2,270.00 was perfect based on the contract that I signed of an annual teaching salary of $4,800.00. I thought I was on my way to experiencing independence.

I continued with my college classes and began thinking of the teaching job. A week before final exams, my brother Lee, Mamá, and

I took the bus to go to Lewisville, north of Dallas, to pick up the car and sign all the papers. I did not drive on the way back. Lee did all the driving. Mamá felt that it was the best thing for all of us. I agreed with her. By now, I was totally stressed, thinking of the last finals I had to pass to get my degree and certification, a new job, a new car, and figuring out how I was going to face Papá about wanting to spend the rest of my life with Juan. I not only had to pass my final exams, I also had to take an oral final exam in speech class with Dr. Arthur Hayes, my speech professor, and an oral English/speech test with Mr. Calder to receive my Texas teacher certification. Dr. Hayes, my speech professor, stressed me out like a shivering mouse stuck in the corner of a room, with no place to go, facing the tomcat positioned for the attack.

In front of him, we, as students, had to "e nun ci ate" every syllable as if he were listening to a movie in slow motion. During his class, I always felt a million butterflies in my stomach and a deep sense of incompetence and failure, like having fallen into a grave pit alive and never being able to crawl out to reach the top. Every sentence I spoke had at least two or three words that I was not pronouncing correctly. He would interrupt me immediately after I uttered the mispronounced word and modeled the correct pronunciation for me to repeat at least three times. I dreaded every minute of his class. Shihuahua . . . no, no, no, Chi Chi, tongue must be curved and touch the palate to pronounce it correctly Chihuahua! I learned to keep trying. Regardless of my feelings of inadequacies with pronunciations, it was the requirement, so I had no choice but to do what was required if I wanted to be certified.

I never had Mr. Calder for any class, but I was very uncomfortable with him because of the way he eyed all the girls from head to toe. He had a reputation of liking all the girls on campus and always managed to figure out a way to hug them. On the advice of several of my girlfriends, I managed never to register for a class with him; but he was the one who gave the oral English/speech test, so I had no choice but to go to his office for the exam. Times like this were when I wish I had Papá right next to me to protect me from dirty old men. I asked Juan to walk me to the office where the test was administered. Mr. Calder knew Juan was outside waiting for me to finish the test. No hanky-panky opportunity allowed with this student!

I was excited about my new car. The first day I had it at home, I drove it to McAllen to do a test run while running some errands. The next day being Saturday, I decided to go to the college library to study for my final exams. I drove, and Imelda and Loreto decided to go with me. I had no problems driving all the way to Edinburg, about a seven-mile drive, until I made a right-hand turn into the entrance to the library. I know I turned the steering wheel to the right all the way; but somehow, I hit a triangle full of gravel, skidded, lost control of the car, and hit head-on the huge light pole dead center. Lee hit his head on the dashboard and had a nosebleed; Imelda, thrown toward the front passenger seat, hit her legs against the back of the seat; and I just sat there with the steering wheel inches from my chest.

Loreto passed out for a few seconds. Shocked and afraid of what had happened, I would not move an inch. What happened? What did I do? The car hood, crushed at the center through the carburetor, looked like someone meticulously designed a pair of wings on it. Before I realized it, I heard the ambulance coming. The library had many windows with a view to the entrance, so many students heard the impact of the crash and looked out the window to see what happened. The ambulance came; and I managed to get out of the car, shaken and wobbly, but with not even a scrape. We were all transported to the hospital and checked out.

Loreto and I were fine, but Imelda had two bruised legs; but thank God, no broken bones! She was very pale, so she bruised easily. How were we going to tell Papá and Mamá what happened? In addition, who was going to tell them? I didn't even know how it all happened. While I stayed with Imelda to make sure she was all right, Loreto decided to call Father John McGrath, the Neumann Club chaplain of the college. Fr. McGrath, OMI, came over to see what had happened and gave us all a blessing. He decided to call Fr. Haile, OMI, in Pharr and asked him to inform Papá and Mamá about the accident. He did and then drove to the Edinburg hospital where we were. Papá and Mamá drove themselves, and they all got there at the same time. Mamá and Papá were a nervous wreck with just the thought that two priests were there praying for us. They expected the worst! Anytime there's a priest with a patient in a hospital, one expects the worst. Fortunately, we were all spared any injuries and released from the hospital within a couple of hours with prescriptions for pain medication and muscle relaxers. We all went home with Papá. I don't really know what went on after we arrived home. I just knew I had to take final exams, and I had to study. I hit the books as soon as I could. I'm not sure I made any progress under the influence of medications and the rerun of the incident in my mind constantly.

The next day, Papá called the car insurance company, and they agreed that the car could be repaired; but it was going to take at least a month to six weeks before I could get it back. The insurance adjuster and mechanics that inspected the car after the accident were in awe at how I survived the accident. There was less than twelve inches between the steering wheel and the seat where I was. The fact that I had a very thin frame and weighed less than a hundred pounds kept me from being crushed to death. Papá agreed to drive me to work when school started, and I continued to ride the bus to college until the end of my final exams. The local Edinburg newspaper and the college paper covered the accident. I was so embarrassed about what happened, that all I wanted to do was finish my exams and get out of college and not have to face one more student asking, "What happened? Did a pole get in your way?" My response with a smile was the same every time: "Yes, a pole got in the way." Some people never realize sarcastic remarks hurt and stay with you for a lifetime.

Somehow, I managed to pass my exams, but in one class, philosophy of education, barely. I thought I had done well when I took the exam, but the professor told me I barely made it. I must have been so drugged from the pain medicines I was on; I had no sense of what was happening. I probably walked around for days looking like a zombie, taking exams and not aware of anything else. Regardless, I was now ready for graduation.

Graduation night came; and Mamá, Loreto, and Imelda attended. Papá decided he did not want to go. He complained about having headaches regularly. So he stayed home. Juan also attended and wanted to take me out for dinner afterward; but, of course, I did not have permission from Papá, so the only celebrating we did after the ceremony was a congratulatory hug and "talk to you later." Not even a kiss! Kissing in public was not an acceptable behavior. That was out of the question.

Juan called me on the phone a week later and again asked me to marry him. This time he was very firm about getting a definite answer and commitment from me so he could begin planning. He was offered a job in Brownsville as a junior accountant with Long, Chilton & Shepherd, a CPA firm, and he wanted to plan moving to Brownsville from Edinburg to begin his career. I said, "Yes, I'll marry you. I only ask that we plan for a wedding a year from now so I can teach for a year and figure out how to deal with Papa's rules." He agreed, and his favorite phrase from that day on was, "Come hell or high water, we're going to get married!"

My First Teaching Job

I only had a week off after graduation before I started my teaching job. Papá was to drive me to Donna in the mornings to work, and whoever was available in the afternoon would pick me up, either he or Loreto Jr. I knew I would not be left at school too late because I still had the duty of fixing dinner every evening for the whole family. By now, Mama's high blood pressure was getting worse, and I still kept up with my daily duties of cooking breakfast and dinner and ironing all of Saturday morning to help her as much as I could. I never figured out why my other sisters never helped in the kitchen. Some evenings I would be so tired and frustrated that I just wanted to run away from it all, but I never had the heart to leave Mamá alone in the kitchen as exhausted and weary as she looked keeping up with the home and Papa's demands.

After just a month of teaching, the district asked me to teach evening classes for adults twice a week. The classes consisted of basic math, reading skills, and vocabulary development. The ten students in the class were all Spanish speakers who had not even attended eight years of school. This was one of my most rewarding experiences I ever had in my life. Here I am, a twenty-one-year-old, teaching men and women old enough to be my parents, and they were so courteous and grateful that I chose to spend my evenings with them instead of doing other things. I admired their sincerity, drive, dedication, and humble spirit. They were so conscientious and meticulously followed every instruction I gave. I grew very fond of several of the women, the three Rodriguez sisters, who attended my class. They shared with me that they were never allowed to finish school because their father was so strict that he took them out of school so they would not get involved with boys. None of them ever married! They just volunteered at church and sang in the choir.

I settled into my day-job routine, learning about my students, their learning needs, and the environment they came from. I loved teaching from day one. The majority of my students could not even afford the seven cents that it cost to buy a milk carton for the midmorning snack. They did without one daily. When I realized the problem, I arranged with the cafeteria personnel for all students in my class to receive their midmorning drink of choice, either white milk or chocolate milk, daily. I personally covered the cost for the students who could not afford it and never informed the cafeteria staff. I just handed in the money needed daily. No one in the cafeteria or any staff members seemed to be concerned about whether the students could afford it or not.

I had one accelerated English language arts class with mostly Anglo students and two Hispanic boys. My other classes were all regular classes and one remedial reading class. Teaching the remedial reading class left me with many concerns daily. I have always felt guilty believing that I did not do any justice to the students in that class. The students were so far behind in their reading skill, vocabulary development, and articulation of the English language, that I sincerely believe that I could not help them much seeing them only an hour a day and having to use the SRA (Student Reading Activities) color-coded reading cards that progressively became more difficult as the students progressed from level to level. They needed one-on-one instruction, and there was never enough time to do individualized tutoring. This was my first awareness of the need for curriculum reform and the need for scheduling additional time for instruction.

By the end of September, my new car was ready for me to pick up. The Ford dealer replaced all damaged parts, and it was again a brand-new car. Papá told me that he was going to pick it up, that he was going to keep it, and I was not allowed to drive it because of what happened. I was devastated; I did not understand why he was so selfish and self-centered and always took care of his wants first. He told me that he and Lee were going to use the car because they needed a second car for Lee and Teresa to go to college. I kept making my monthly payments on the car, the car insurance, and even paid all of their monthly gasoline bills because Papá asked me to let him have my gasoline credit card, and he never returned it to me. He used it to fill up not only my car but also his, as he needed to. The bills came in monthly in my name, and I had no choice but to pay them.

Imelda decided to look for a job also before my graduation. She found a job in Relámpago, a little county district, located south of Mercedes. The very small county districts had a very difficult time finding personnel because their pay scales were very low. They also only required sixty hours of college work and did not require certification. Imelda did not have a degree but had the sixty hours of coursework that was required for hiring. So now, there were two of us with teaching jobs, Lee and Teresa were attending college, and Papá was continuing with his packing-shed work, which became less and less lucrative as times began to change. Machinery began taking the place of the crop pickers. Packing sheds also became more automated and needed fewer laborers. Papa began to struggle with these changes in front of him, but this was all he knew how to do, so he continued with the same field of work.

By now, I'm feeling like I'm being stomped on. I was respectful, never disagreed, nor answered Papá back, and too scared of his unpredictable, reactive behaviors to even consider taking a stand on what I thought were my rights. In addition, I now wanted to get married, and how in the world was I going to deal with Papá and his unreasonable behaviors if I spoke against his decision not to let me have my car? 'Tis better to keep it all inside and just deal with it. Again, I just accepted his orders and went to my room, cried out of frustration, and talked myself into accepting Papa's commands and the commandment of honoring thy father and thy mother.

As usual, I escaped the stress that Papá created by concentrating on my schoolwork and chores at home. Within a couple of weeks, I learned that a married couple that was also teaching at Moye Junior High had to drive through Pharr to get to their apartment in McAllen. In conversation, I mentioned about my transportation problem, merely sharing generalities and not the true story of Papa's decisions. I had learned, from my high school experiences and Papa's reaction to that system, to share with adults outside the family only the important message needed to be conveyed, and not all the horrid details of Papa's reactive and unpredictable personality that was so complex and difficult to understand by family members, let alone outsiders. They offered to pick me up in the morning and drop me off in the afternoon after school. I arranged to pay them a weekly fee for the carpool. At least with this arrangement, I was free from having to depend on Papá or anyone else in the family for transportation.

Guess Who's Coming to Visit

The last week in September, without any warning, Juan shows up at the church bingo held every Sunday late afternoon, which I, along with several of my sisters, would attend to help with the sales. My birthday, on the twenty-second, was in the middle of the week; and we did not see each other because of our work schedules—he, now living in Brownsville, sixty miles from Pharr, a full hour's drive. Juan found me amongst the crowd on the church grounds and handed me a birthday gift—a Timex watch that had five different colored bands and five round matching face discs to change according to what you were wearing for the day. I was so impressed! I could not believe it! For a poor working guy from Raymondville, this must have been a major decision to spend that kind of money on a gift for a girlfriend.

He stayed until the bingo was over, and I walked home as usual with all of my sisters. I had no idea of Juan's plans. I thought he was driving back to Brownsville immediately after our visit.

To my amazement, I had not been home more than ten minutes when he shows up at our front door, ringing the doorbell. Papá saw him from his bedroom, immediately went to the door, and asked him what he wanted through the screen door. Juan responded with, "I've come to visit with Carmen." Papás response was, "Tu no tienes negocio con Carmen y aquí no se va a meter ningún cabrón" (You have no business with Carmen and no SOB is going to enter this house). As Lee is parking the car in the front of the house, Papá opens the screen door, confronts Juan with a square body, and begins to yell every imaginable cussword in Spanish, ordering Juan to leave his property. Lee runs up the steps to the porch, positions himself between Juan and Papá, and asks, "What's going on here?" Papá responds with, "This SOB wants to see Carmen and he has no business with her in this house." Lee turns to Juan, asks him to leave, and tells him that he will talk to Papá about his request to see Carmen. I rushed to my room as Juan left and witnessed all the commotion by peeking through the living room door. Papá storms into the house and yells, "Carmen, come here!" My stomach is churning, and I'm almost shivering, fearing what I had to face now. I immediately went to the living room, and he asked me, "¿Qué negocio tiene ese muchacho contigo?" (What business does that boy have with you?)

"Papá, he doesn't have any business with me. He just wants to visit with me because he wants to be my boyfriend and I want him to be my boyfriend."

He came back with a loud, emphatic order: "You do not have permission to have a boyfriend and he will not step in this house . . . he's nothing but a Mexican Indian . . . what kind of people are you wanting to hang around with? Dime con quien andas y te diré quien eres (You can judge a man by the company he keeps). We are Spaniards coming from a long line of blue bloods and no Mexican Indian is going to invade my house."

It was not the first time I heard about our "blue blood" ancestry claim. He reminded all of us about it every opportunity he had. Yes, if our looks were the indicator that determined our "blue blood" origins, then definitely at least four (Imelda, Loreto Jr., Margarita, and Enrique) of the eleven offspring definitely were born with very pale white skin that showed the very blue superficial veins supposedly distinguishing the difference between an upper-class family and a working-class one. I turned out middle of the road, a blend of Mama's olive skin and his very pale skin. If this was so important to him, why did he marry an olive-skinned Italian woman? Maybe he did not realize it, but he had already broken the tight-knit circle of the Spanish family genealogy by marrying Mamá, an Italian olive-skinned woman.

I just stood there, listened to his angry tone and hurtful words, and realized how prejudiced he was against any dark-skinned Mexican-looking Indian wanting to become romantically involved with one of his daughters. I went to my room even more determined to win this battle somehow. I suppose "My Heart Has a Mind of Its Own," and now I was even more determined to pursue my heart's need.

Lee and I discussed who could possibly convince Papá to start listening to my wishes. We decided that the only person in the whole world he would listen to was Fr. Smith, now residing in Brownsville as the chaplain at the Villa Maria campus where I had attended my first year of high school. He was now retired and celebrated Mass daily for the Sisters of the Incarnate Word who were in charge of the campus and kept a vegetable garden as a hobby. He also suffered from a severe case of shingles during an era when there were no medications to relieve his discomfort. He lived with pain daily. Papá looked up to Fr. Smith with respect since he knew him as a very young boy and had been taught how to fish and hunt by him.

A few days later, Lee decided to drive to Brownsville to speak with Fr. Smith and share the story of Juan's wishes to marry me and Papa's unwillingness to accept him. Fr. Smith's response was, "It takes hitting him in the head with a two by four just to get his attention. I will definitely go to talk to him, but I need transportation to get there and be brought back to Brownsville." Fr. Smith knew Juan's family because as a younger priest he had served as pastor of Our Lady of Guadalupe Catholic Church in Raymondville located just a block from where Juan grew up.

Another one of Juan's stories about his growing-up years in Raymondville dealt with his attending catechism classes with the nuns, who were all Mexican. He was always trying to figure out a way to get out of attending the classes. One Sunday morning, Juan arrived very late because he stopped to play marbles with the neighborhood boys who did not attend church. On the way to the class, Fr. Smith stopped him to lecture him about the importance of getting to class on time. Juan had his face down looking on the ground throughout the lecture. After a couple of minutes of not listening, Juan asks Fr. Smith, "I bet you can't tell me how many ants have gone into that hole on the ground?" He ran to class immediately!

Lee called Juan and asked him to visit with Fr. Smith to arrange for the first attempt at convincing Papá to change his mind about allowing Juan to come and visit me at home. Juan made the appointment and visited with Fr. Smith. I had already spoken with Juan about a possible day for Fr. Smith to come visit, and I picked the third Sunday in October in the afternoon when the annual church bazaar was taking place. I volunteered to run the cakewalk all afternoon, so I knew I was not going to be home, and I did everything I knew on how to avoid being around Papá especially during times when I knew his reaction was going to be verbally volatile. They decided that Juan would drive him to our home and drop him off to visit with Papá while Juan visited with me at the bazaar. Papá did not know that Fr. Smith was coming over, so he was very surprised to see him unannounced. However, since he was a close family friend, he was always welcomed at any time.

When Juan and I arrived home after six in the evening, Papá and Fr. Smith were sitting in the living room, chatting. Papá gave me a vicious stare but did not say a word. Papá ordered Juan to sit down at the dining table with me while they finished their conversation. Fr. Smith told Papá that Juan was going to visit weekly and that some Sundays he would come with him to join us for dinner. Papá accepted it, kept his silence, and did not speak to me all week.

Mamá shared with me later that Fr. Smith told Papá he could no longer keep me from making decisions about my future. He had to learn to let go. I was no longer a child. I knew what I wanted and should be allowed to get married if that is what I chose to do. Fr. Smith made a deal with Juan that evening. Juan was to pick him up weekly, on Wednesdays, and take him out for dinner at his favorite Mexican restaurant, Lavios, in Brownsville. Juan agreed and made it a weekly event. They would arrive at the restaurant by six in the evening, have a meal, and sit and converse until the restaurant closed after 9:00 p.m. Fr. Smith smoked a cigar and would ask for a shot of tequila, dip the cigar in the tequila, and enjoyed the puffing all evening long. I witnessed that at our home also, so I was very aware of his habit with the cigar.

The weekly visits began with Fr. Smith and Juan arriving early enough for Juan and I to walk to Sunday evening Mass. I would prepare dinner before his arrival. We would attend Mass, come home, and have dinner with Mamá at the table. Papá never joined us. He just sat in the living room, conversed with Fr. Smith, and they watched TV, ignoring us while we conversed. I was fine with that and happy that we were making progress. Juan left by 8:30 p.m. for his hour drive back to Brownsville. Fr. Smith had to be back at his living quarters before ten in the evening because the nuns locked the entrance gate to the grounds precisely at ten.

The Asking of the Hand in Marriage

By mid-November, Juan approached Papá during one of the visits and informed him that his parents wanted to come and ask for my hand in marriage. Traditionally, asking for the bride's hand in marriage was actually asking the parents to give permission for the marriage to take place and to bless the union. Papá never answered him, so Juan told him he was bringing them the following week. I had never spoken to his parents. I had seen them once at his graduation and then at George's wedding, but not interacted with them. I had no idea what I was supposed to do during this visit, nor did I know what formalities were to be followed for this event. Do we invite them over for dinner? Or do we just offer them some coffee and dessert? Either one of those choices would have been the courteous thing to do. In addition, we were always taught that practicing our courtesies when interacting with people was very important, and there was never an excuse for not practicing them at all times. Papá suggested nothing. Therefore, I decided just to have coffee and cookies ready to offer them.

On the Sunday before Thanksgiving, in the afternoon, Juan drove from Brownsville to Raymondville, a sixty-mile drive, to pick up his parents and drive them to Pharr, an additional sixty-mile drive. His parents arrived and were greeted with a handshake. Mamá was pleasant as usual. Papá, with a stern firm look, as if he were inspecting every visible feature they possessed, asked them to sit down. Yes, they looked very different from our family. His father, Gustavo Moreno Sr., was small in stature, no more than five feet eight inches tall. He was very light skinned with very light grey eyes; after all, he was of Spanish background. On the other hand, his mother, Sofia Muñoz Moreno, was a large very brown-skinned matronly looking woman with very distinct indigenous Indian-looking features. She projected a strong dominant personality, and it seemed to me that Papá had probably met his match.

Neither Mamá nor Juan's mother said anything. His father, who spoke only Spanish, began with, "Mi hijo Juan me dice que quiere casarse con su hija Carmen. Para nosotros es un honor venir a pedirle la mano de su hija para que se case con nuestro hijo Juan. Le aseguro que mi hijo tiene solamente buenas intenciones y le pedimos que les de su bendición para que se preparen para su matrimonio. Venemos de familias pobres, pero le aseguro con mi palabra que somos sinceros con esta súplica y esperamos que les conceda su bendición" (My son Juan tells me that he would like to marry your daughter Carmen. For us, it is an honor to come here and ask for her hand in marriage to our son Juan. I assure you that my son has only honorable intentions and we ask you for your blessing so they can prepare for marriage. We come from poor families, but I assure you with my word that we are sincere with this request and we hope that you grant them your blessing). I was so impressed with my future father-in-law's articulation of the formal Spanish language that I wondered if all parents who went through this custom memorized the request prior to the visit.

Papás response was, "Pues lo voy a pensar y les contesto después (Well, I will think about it and let you know later). He changed the conversation immediately by asking questions about where they were from and where they lived. The men did all the talking. Don Gustavo shared that they were originally from Los Saenz, Texas, a *ranchito* next to Roma, Texas.

Roma-Los Saenz is two adjoining communities directly across from Ciudad Miguel Alemán, Tamaulipas, Mexico, in southwestern Starr County in the lower Rio Grande Valley. It was part of Mexico until 1948, when it became a part of the United States after Mexico ceded a large territory when the signing of the Treaty of Guadalupe Hidalgo ended the Mexican-American War. The inhabitants of that area were all Mexicans, living north of the Rio Grande River, until the signing of the treaty, when the Rio Grande River became the dividing line between the United States and Mexico. The lifestyles of the inhabitants of the area did not change. Their livelihood consisted of cattle ranching and agriculture, mostly melons. The only thing that changed was the borders; now they became citizens of the United States of America.

Papa began name-dropping, which was one of his favorite tactics to use when trying to impress anyone about his knowledge of people. Mamá and Doña Sofia just listened. The visit lasted only about half an hour. I offered them some cookies, but they graciously said, "No, gracias." They had had a full lunch and were still digesting it but were very grateful for the offer.

As soon as the formal handshakes (no hugs) were done, they left, and I walked away from the living room as fast as I could. That strategy did not work. Papá immediately calls me and starts with, "¿Sabes quien manda en esa familia?" (Do you know who's boss in that family?)

"No, Papa, I don't know because I don't know them."

"Well, I'm telling you right now, she's the boss in that family. The man of that household probably has no say about anything," was Papa's observation. "What kind of family are you getting yourself involved with? The man should be the *jefe* of the house, not the woman. You want to get yourself into this kind of family? Think about it, she looks like a pure Mexican Indian. Que tontería!" (What nonsense!)

I did not answer, just listened, and left it at that. A couple of days later, after I came home from work, he again summoned me to the living room. He tells me he had driven to Raymondville to look at the home where

Juan's family lived. He found out that they are very poor; there was no way he had anything to offer me for my future. The home in Raymondville was about a fourth the size of our home, made of very light green siding, just like many of the homes in our neighborhood. The house was bought as a shell with only exterior walls because that was all the family could afford. As the father acquired money by working as a ranch hand, he added a hall and divided the inside of the house into three small rooms. One bedroom was for all four boys and one bedroom for the parents. The living room was small, and the other half of the house was the kitchen and dining room. The neighborhood where he lived did not have sidewalks or a drainage system. The homes did not have carpet grass. Yes, it was a poor neighborhood, just like ours, but our home was much larger and better built than the average home in the neighborhood.

Papá was obviously looking for what kind of dowry he would offer me, as that was also another custom in the Spanish tradition. A dowry was the least of my concerns. We both had our education, and I believed we could make a life together with both of us working in our professions. I told him Juan had an education and was already on his way to having a professional career and that I knew he was going to be successful. That is all I needed. He accused me of being *caprichuda* (making a decision on a whim). "Puro capricho!" was his comment. All right, I suppose that if being *caprichuda* is what it takes to get there, I certainly am that!

Juan continued with his weekly visits, now coming by himself at times without Fr. Smith. Since his father told Papá that Juan's intentions were honorable, Juan knew he had to behave with me and not demonstrate any type of behaviors that showed disrespect of any kind. In other words, he had to keep his hands off me!

For Thanksgiving, Juan brought Fr. Smith to spend the afternoon with us and have dinner. Of course, Juan had to join us also. In front of Fr. Smith, Papá was always as courteous as he could be. The day went smoothly, with Papá having no major outbursts at any time. We had the traditional turkey meal with all the trimmings and enjoyed it.

On the first Sunday in December, Juan asked Papá for an answer about his parents' request for my hand in marriage. Papá told Juan to bring them back to the house in a month and that he would speak to them at that time. Juan answered him with a firm, "No, I'm not bringing them back for an answer. You can answer me right here. Bringing them over here is very difficult because I have to travel a lot making the rounds from Brownsville to Raymondville, then from Raymondville to Pharr and then back to Raymondville and back to Brownsville." Papá gave him his vicious stare but never answered. I was surprised Juan responded in such an assertive way and Papá did not go off on one of his verbal outbursts, as he would do with me.

That day Juan informed Papá that he was planning to give me a ring for Christmas and planned to bring it to me on the Sunday before Christmas. Fr. Haile ordered our rings, a three-piece set, through a wholesale catalog that he used for shopping. I had picked the set I liked, and Fr. Haile made several phone calls to the shippers, asking all sorts of questions to assure us that we were getting a quality diamond with our purchase. The set was a very simple quarter-carat solitaire diamond and two wedding bands. Juan had already paid him for the rings. I never told Papá about where Juan had purchased the rings.

Papa Gustavo Moreno and Mama Sofia Munoz Moreno

The Engagement

The Sunday before Christmas came, and Juan arrived for his visit earlier than usual. Papá knew that the ring was coming, so he was ready for Juan when he arrived. He asked him to sit at one end of the sofa. Then Papá sat next to him and asked me to sit at the other end of the sofa. Mamá sat in the recliner chair by herself. Is this the way a couple who are about to be engaged supposed to sit? With the papá between them? I had never done this before, so maybe this was the way it was supposed to be. The movies on TV never showed it like this!

Juan began by telling Papá that he cared for me and wanted to present me with the *anillo de compromiso* (ring of commitment). He also told him that we wanted to start planning our future together, and we were looking forward to our wedding day. Papá took the ring from Juan's hand, looked at it, and handed it to me. I placed the ring on the fourth finger of my left hand as they both watched my own personal ritual. Inside me, every nerve in my body was ecstatically clapping, witnessing the progress made and now being one more step closer to walking down the aisle to the altar. No hug, no kiss, no good wishes from either Papá or Mamá, no nothing. Just Papá between us!

All my brothers and sisters were in the back bedrooms listening attentively as they had done with every other event involving Juan. I could sense their excitement about the event, but they were all careful not to show any sort of happiness for me for fear of Papa's reaction.

Again, dinner was already done, so it was time for us to walk to church and attend our usual Sunday Mass. The gospel reading for the day was the Gospel of St. John 2:1-11, when the power of Jesus is manifested at the wedding at Cana. Jesus performed His first miracle at the request of His mother, Mary. How fitting was this on our engagement day? I reflected on that gospel all week, believing that I had already experienced a miracle by just having an engagement ring on my finger.

After Mass, we showed Fr. Haile the ring on my hand. He was thrilled and asked us to let him know when we wanted to set the date for the wedding so he could prepare us for it. He knew a wedding was now in the planning. We walked home; and I served Juan, Mama, and myself dinner. We ate and chatted, and he left at the usual time. I walked him to the door and left him with a big smile. He did it! One more step accomplished on this bumpy journey.

After the engagement event, no one in the family thought much about it because Mamá and Papa's twenty-fifth wedding anniversary, on February 23, 1966, was the next major event that all of us were looking forward to celebrating. They decided to have a Mass of thanksgiving, with a renewal of vows, at St. Margaret's Church, followed by a reception and banquet at the McAllen Civic Center. Mamá generated the list of invitees immediately after Christmas, and plans got under way for the celebration. During the next two months, all conversations at home revolved around the twenty-fifth anniversary celebration. It was very important for Papá not to forget to invite all the influential *politicos* that he knew and all of their *compadres* that both of my parents had connections with for the past twenty-five years. Becoming a *compadre* created a lifelong bond between couples and was taken very seriously. A couple became your compadre and comadre whenever a couple stood as *padrinos*, godparents, during the receiving of a sacrament. In both the Spanish and Italian culture, there is no greater honor than to be asked to be a *madrina* (godmother) or a *padrino* (godfather). Their role was to share in the parenting of the child, and especially in support of educating the child in the practice of the Catholic faith. They were godparents to many, many children in the barrio. I was always amazed when a child from the neighborhood would see Papá and Mamá at church and approach them, greeting each of them with a kiss in the hand. Each one of us children had at least one godparent, and some of us, more than one. It is customary to have a godparent for baptism, confirmation, First Communion, and, ultimately, marriage. Papá picked our godparents, always keeping in mind their position and level of influence in the community. My *padrinos*, Eduardo and Panchita Vela, were from Hidalgo. He was the mayor of Hidalgo for many, many years. They were my godparents for my baptism, confirmation, and first Holy Communion. I did not see them often but spoke to my *madrina* occasionally on the phone.

Papá became excited just adding people to the list. Every day he thought of one more name to add to the invitee list. By the time all the relatives' names along with all of the compadres and the acquaintances they had through church and political involvement were added, the list grew to more than two hundred names. This was definitely going to be a big event.

Again, Juan's assignment for the celebration was to drive Fr. Smith to Pharr for the Mass and the reception. The Solemn High Mass was cocelebrated by Fr. Haile, OMI, as the main celebrant and Fr. Smith, OMI; and Fr. Barrett, OMI, our assistant pastor, was assisting.

Juan played his role as expected and sat at one of the many tables prepared for the two hundred guests that attended the celebration. All the priests along with the family members sat at the head table; Juan, not being a part of the family, did not join us at the head table.

An official photographer, Luis Garcia, from the local newspaper, the *Valley Evening Monitor*, covered the reception held at the McAllen Civic Center. The description of the event and a picture of Mamá and Papá appeared in the Sunday edition of the newspaper the following weekend, March 6, 1966. Papá was happy!

Papa and Mama in 1958

Pre-Cana Sessions

Now that the twenty-fifth wedding anniversary celebration was over, I could begin to concentrate on wedding plans in between my day teaching job, teaching night classes for adults, and volunteer organ playing at church. After Easter, Fr. Haile reminded me that we had to start planning for a time when he could meet with both Juan and me to prepare us for marriage. The classes were called Pre-Cana sessions, and we had to have at least six sessions with him prior to marriage. On a typical Sunday evening after Mass, Fr. Haile suggested we just stay after Mass and visit with him to begin our sessions. Why not? We decided to join him in the rectory after Mass and begin our sessions.

After the session, we walked home as usual, except we were an hour and a half late returning from church. Papá was waiting for us but did not question us on our lateness. We proceeded with our usual dinner at the dining room table with Mamá joining us. After Juan left, Papá summoned me with his very recognizable tone of disapproval of something.

He starts with, "Why were you so late coming home from church today? Where did you go?"

"Papá, we didn't go anywhere. We were with Fr. Haile speaking to him." "What kind of business do you have with Fr. Haile that takes an hour to talk about?" he continued with his questioning.

"Papá, we stayed to talk to Fr. Haile so he can prepare us for marriage. We started the Pre-Cana classes today in preparation for our marriage."

He continued with his questions, "What is Pre-Cana?"

"Those are the classes that Juan and I have to attend to prepare ourselves for getting married," I responded.

He responds with a loud stern tone, "I have never given you permission to get married. I will impose a *plazo* of one year before you can get married." (A *plazo* was the custom of imposing a length of time decided by the parents of the bride. During this period, the bride is to discern if she really wanted to marry the beau.)

Just hearing the word *plazo* made my stomach churn even more. I knew what that meant! He probably wanted me to give up on the crazy idea of mine that I wanted to marry this *indio*. My mind was thinking faster than I could process all my thoughts. I had done all he expected of me; I asked for permission for Juan to come visit me at home. I followed every rule he imposed on us as far as dating was concerned, had Juan's parents ask for my hand in marriage, never went anywhere with Juan except to church and straight home afterward, and now a *plazo* . . . I don't think so!

I took a deep breath and said words I never thought could come out of my mouth . . . "Papá, on August 7 of this year, Juan and I are going to get married at St. Margaret's Church down the street at four in the afternoon. If you would like to walk me down the aisle, I would appreciate that very much. If you do not want to do that, I will have Loreto Jr. or Tío Alex walk me down the aisle of the church. Juan and I have begun to make our wedding plans and that's the way it's going to be."

As he stared at me, he asks, "What are you telling me?" "Papá, you heard me, and that's all I have to say."

"Grosera!" he responded. "No tienes nada de respeto a tu padre." (Rude! You have no respect for your father.)

If my response was disrespectful, then I suppose I was breaking the commandment to honor my father and my mother. I was definitely at a saturation point and felt I had had enough of Papa's demands. I left him standing there and went to my bedroom to reflect on my lack of respect for Papá. I heard him summon Mamá and started complaining to her about my disrespectful nature toward him. Papá ignored me for the next month and did not say a word to me even when I was fixing him dinner or serving him. Somehow, by now, I had grown a protective shell thicker than that of a fifty-year-old tortoise, which helped me stay focused on my dream of walking down the aisle. I just took it in stride and managed somehow to tell myself to stay focused on the wedding plans.

The Trousseau

Many times throughout my growing years, I admired Mama's cedar chest filled with her wedding dress, headpiece, and school memorabilia from her years prior to marriage.

About once a year, usually during the summer when school was not in session and we had time to converse, she would open her chest and show us girls her wedding dress. I suppose it was a time for her to reminisce of her carefree years of no responsibility, just herself and her teaching. She glowed proudly as she told us that her dress came from the East Coast through a catalog order. Unlike the traditional Mexican wedding dresses that were covered with wax flowers all over even on the train and headpieces, hers was made totally of very, very fine silky chiffon, yards and yards of it with a very long train and a very simple headpiece made of silk. I suppose this was Mama's opportunity to exhibit her bragging rights since in the era of the '30s, women sewed all their clothing. Not much clothing was store-bought, especially for women. I often wondered if Mamá Grande ever approved of the dress. Again, I realized that Mamá did not have the same tastes as the Treviño women.

I had made a decision since my high school sewing years that if I ever got married, I would sew my own dress. Now came the time for me to act on that decision. I began by looking at the Simplicity and *McCall's* patterns at the fabric shops in McAllen. I found a pattern that not only had the pattern for the dress but also the pattern for the headpiece. I decided to get it and called Juan to give him the estimate of the cost of the dress. Traditionally, according to what Mamá told me, the groom is to provide the bride with a dowry, an amount of money, which would cover the cost of the wedding gown and all of her personal needs for the wedding day. However, my Anglo girlfriends told me that this custom was the total opposite of their traditions.

The following weekend, during his routine visit, Juan brought me a $100 check for the wedding dress expenses. I told Mamá about the money and about my decision to make the dress and headpiece.

I still do not know what possessed me to buy a dress pattern that had thirty-five loop buttonholes all along the back of the dress and five at the end of each of the long sleeves that tapered to a point toward the middle finger of the hand. I had enough money to buy the peau de soie fabric for the dress and the headpiece. The headpiece was a very simple flower with three leaves laying flat at the bottom of the flower. I followed the basic pattern and added my own design as I began to sew.

Mamá kept her sewing machine in our bedroom along the wall by the door entrance. This was convenient for her during our school hours. She could keep all her sewing materials away from all the children after they came home from school. I began working on it as soon as school was out in early June and finished it in six weeks. This project became a challenge only because of the thirty-five loop buttonholes and covered buttons that ran all down the back of the dress past the waistline. As I began sewing, there were days when I wondered if I could ever get all those button loops in correctly and straight. It was a challenge, but I seem to thrive on challenges. I also decided to add decorative trim along the edge of the train and throughout the bodice of the dress, all of which had to be hand sewn. I worked on the dress daily until it was finished.

Papá began to speak to me after seeing me spend all of my time in my bedroom, sewing. Maybe by now he realized I was not changing my mind and even if he thought of imposing a *plazo*, I was not going to follow that demand.

I had a picture taken and submitted it to the *Valley Evening Monitor* in McAllen, announcing my formal engagement to Juan. Papá now knew that the engagement announcement appeared in the newspaper that was delivered to our home daily, and I was only looking forward.

He reminded me that on the list for invitees to the wedding, I must not forget all of the family members from Montemorelos, Mexico, and all of his political friends who were the local judges. I assured him that I would review the list with Mamá before mailing any invitations. Somehow, I thought, he seemed to begin accepting my decision to marry.

Los Padrinos

Traditionally, the godparents, *los padrinos*, play a very important role in the spiritual development of the child they are to sponsor. In our family, our parents chose our godparents, even for weddings. They always picked influential members of the community, not necessarily the ones who lived in Pharr, but anyone they were acquainted with who lived in the Valley from Brownsville to McAllen. They all had to be practicing Catholics, and Papá always reminded us that they, as we, were all Democrats, and the men were usually members of the Knights of Columbus council, a Catholic men's organization that he belonged to in the McAllen council.

For our wedding, we would have three couples as padrinos. The most important couple known as the *primeros padrinos* will be the first witnesses for the ceremony. Their role continues to be to support the couple in their spiritual development throughout the marriage. In addition, their gift to the bride is to present her with the wedding cake for the reception. The padrinos decided the type of cake they would get; the only question they had for the bride was, "What are the colors that you've chosen for the wedding?" Since I had only one set of padrinos for my baptism, confirmation, and Holy Communion, I knew who would be the first ones asked to be the primeros padrinos for my wedding. My padrinos, Eduardo Vela Sr. and his wife Francisca, lived in Hidalgo where he served as mayor of the City of Hidalgo for many years. Papá decided he would call them and again invite them to be my godparents at my wedding. "Compadre, su ahijada, Carmen, dice que se quiere casar con el muchacho Juan Moreno de Raymondville . . . haber, ¿qué vamos hacer con estos jóvenes?" (Compadre, your goddaughter, Carmen, says she wants to marry this boy Juan Moreno from Raymondville . . . let's see, what can we do with these young ones?) Of course, the response was always, "Si, compadre, con mucho gusto, es un placer y honor casar a los jóvenes" (Of course, compadre, it is always a pleasure and honor to marry the young ones). Papá told me that he had a list of the padrinos that I was to ask to sponsor me. I reminded him that Juan also had a say in who the sponsors would be and that I was not going to make all the decisions for the padrinos.

The *padrinos de arras* predominantly practiced in the Hispanic culture present the groom with a small box containing thirteen gold coins. The thirteen coins represent Christ and his twelve disciples. After the marriage vows have been exchanged, the groom presents the *arras* to the bride as a symbol of his readiness to provide financial support in their married life. It also symbolizes good financial stewardship of the household. The bride promises the groom to use the coins wisely. Papá chose Mr. Joe Chapa, a wealthy rancher and influential politician from Edinburg, and his wife Elodia for our *padrinos de arras*.

The only padrinos that Juan picked, besides the three groomsmen, were the *padrinos de lazo*. The *lazo* is a wedding rosary that symbolizes the union of the couple through prayer. The wedding rosary is actually two individual and complete rosaries that meet and become one before the crucifix at the center. It is placed on the couple by the padrinos at the beginning of the celebration of the Eucharist and removed after the Communion service, and the priest gives a final blessing to the bride and groom. Juan chose Arturo Flores and his wife for our *padrinos de lazo*.

Arturo was a certified public accountant, owner of his own business in Edinburg, who had hired Juan as a junior accountant before Juan received his degree. Juan continued working with him until he received an offer in September of 1965 from Long, Chilton & Shepherd, a certified public accounting firm that audited many of the businesses in Brownsville.

To minimize personal expenses, many Hispanic weddings have huge wedding parties. Each additional set of padrinos sponsors an item the bride or groom does not want to pay for. Some of these items include the cushions the bride and groom use to kneel on during the ceremony. Other item may be the veil for the bride, the goblets for toasting, the knife for cutting the wedding cake, and even sponsors for musicians used at the reception. Papá and Mamá always believed that having that many padrinos was an indicator that the groom's family could not afford the wedding. They also reminded us that none of the additional padrinos were connected spiritually to any Catholic traditions.

This was not acceptable in our family, so my wedding party will consist of only the traditional padrinos representing the traditional customs that included specific prayers that the priest would say to bless the items that had a religious significance. I wanted my wedding to be as simple as possible, so I agreed with them on following all the traditional customs regarding padrinos.

Simply, my older sister Imelda will be my maid of honor; Bertita, my cousin from Brownsville, will be my madrina for the missal and rosary; and a college friend, Zelma, will be the only bridesmaid not representing a religious custom. I never told Papá that Zelma was not Catholic. She bought me the wedding album as a gift for being my bridesmaid. I also wanted Peggy, my best friend during my college years, to be part of my wedding party, but she had already moved to a suburb outside of Houston and was unable to attend.

Juan asked three of his college friends to be part of the wedding party. Beto, his college buddy, will be his best man, and two other college buddies—Joe Longoria (Rosie) and Noe Sanchez, a friend from where Juan was born in Los Saenz, Texas—will be groomsmen.

Wedding Lazo

Wedding missal, rosary, and arras.

The Day at Last

I wanted a simple wedding. Nevertheless, a simple wedding seemed to me like it still involved too many details. The wedding padrinos and madrinas had all been asked to sponsor us. I had sewn the wedding dress, veil, and going-away suit. They were ready, hanging in the closet, begging to be worn. Juan and I decided that the reception would be held at the tearoom of the Fairway Motor Hotel in McAllen. The hotel had a large enough room in case three hundred guests showed up. The wedding list of invitees grew daily as Papá kept adding names to the list. We printed three hundred invitations for both sides of the families. Juan only asked for fifty, and my family used the rest. During this era, wedding invitations did not include a request for an RSVP date because wedding receptions consisted merely of serving wedding cake, *pan de polvo* (the traditional Mexican good-luck wedding cookie), ginger ale-lime sherbet punch, coffee, mints, and peanuts. That was it! We did not even plan to have alcohol at the reception!

All of a sudden, the comadres from the barrio who knew me since I was born informed Mamá that they wanted to give me a wedding shower. Before I realized it, I had three showers that I was to attend as an honoree. These beautiful dark-skinned caring, nurturing comadres from the barrio planned a miscellaneous shower in early July at St. Margaret's Parish Hall. I am sure Fr. Haile let them have the hall without charging them a penny. He knew the poverty level that many of them experienced daily. They personally did all the cooking for the evening shower, the baking, and decorating. The comadres had seen me grow up right before their eyes. They were there during all the *tamaladas* (tamale-making gatherings) held at our garage in the back of the house. They were the ones who brought *caldo de pollo* (chicken soup) for the family when Papá Grande and Mamá Grande died or after Mamá gave birth to another baby. They sang at church as I accompanied them with my organ playing many, many times during the years especially during October, the month dedicated to the Rosary, and May, the month dedicated to our Blessed Mother. All services were held in Spanish, and all hymns were sung in Spanish. I was always amazed at their singing voices, always projecting every note with a strong confident outburst as if they knew God appreciated them for using the talents He gave them even though they were never formally educated in reading music. Somehow, they always harmonized beautifully and managed to touch the innermost depth of my soul with their voices. Almost one hundred of the barrio residents attended! How could I have been so fortunate? Can I ever forget these "Dear Hearts and Gentle People" who demonstrated a true labor of love? Never! Doña Pepita decided that she would make all the *pan de polvo* that we needed for the wedding reception. Her little two-room home must have smelled of cinnamon baking for days since she made more than five hundred cookies!

In mid-July, the wedding-party madrinas hosted a miscellaneous shower at the Citrus Room of the Texan Hotel in downtown Pharr. About fifty guests attended that shower, a very different crowd compared to the previous shower. The guests for this shower were the wives of the politicos that Mamá and Papá knew. Since it was held in a THE only nice hotel that Pharr had, the setting was more formal than the first shower. Food was ordered, the cake came from a bakery, the flowers were real, and the hostesses paid for the use of the room. We all spoke English, so the conversations revolved around future prospects for Juan's job and future and my teaching job. Another beautiful caring labor of love demonstrated with a strong Anglo-American influence. I felt so fortunate!

A very small personal shower hosted by the Rodriquez, a family from Donna that I had met through my night teaching job there, was the last bridal shower held in their home. During this era, we did not register in any stores for gifts. Couples did not ask for any gifts. We were grateful for whatever we received. Bathroom towels, kitchen towels, sheets, pillowcases, kitchen appliances, wall decorations, dishes, pots, and pans will all be used after marriage even if the colors did not match or coordinate with anything. This type of decorating, known as "early marriage" décor, was prevalent during this era.

Juan was still in the army reserve and met with the reserves for training one weekend every month. He also had a commitment to attend two weeks of reserve training annually during the first two weeks in July. Even though he was gone during my first shower, his mother attended the shower with the help of his younger brother Noe, who drove her to Pharr for the event. Even though his father owned a pickup truck, transportation was a big issue with his family because there was not necessarily enough money to buy the gasoline needed to drive to Pharr, a 120-mile round-trip to Raymondville.

I had not seen where we were going to live, nor did I have any idea where the home was located in Brownsville. In June, Juan found a home out in the country to rent. It was an unbelievable deal even for 1966—a two-bedroom wood-framed fully furnished home with a living room, dining area, fully equipped kitchen with refrigerator, stove, and one bathroom for $75.00 a month. It even had connections in an outside storage room for a washer and dryer. The home belonged to an elderly couple, the Hoovers, who had used it as their first home but had built a very modest home next door and now used this home as a rental for additional income. The reason the home was completely furnished was because it was usually rented to couples known as "snowbirds" who migrated from the cold winters of the Midwest to South Texas for relief.

Juan explained to the Hoovers that we would probably not want to keep the linens or the kitchen dishes during our rental tenure with them. They were fine with his request.

As soon as Juan returned from his two-week training camp, he asked me to go see the house. I asked Papá if I could go, and he said the only way I could go was if Juan came and picked Mamá and I up and drive us to Brownsville. Papá did not want to have anything to do with it and did not offer to drive me. Again, another message that he still did not approve of this ever-so-close pending union. Juan decided to come over on a Sunday afternoon and pick up Mamá and myself for the ride to Brownsville. We rode in his non-air-conditioned '55 Ford in the middle of the afternoon. It was a typical hot summer day in Texas! I always worried about how the heat affected Mama's high blood pressure. She seemed to handle the hour drive well.

The home was located on Old 77 Highway. It resembled country living with at least a half acre of green lawn in front of the home and between the other two homes on each side of the house. There was no neighborhood for at least five miles from that location. Once during one of our many conversations while visiting on the college campus, Juan brought up the topic of living or not living near his mother after he got married. He said that his rule was going to be that when he got married he had to live at least sixty miles from his mother's home. I asked, "Why?" "I just want to make sure she doesn't check in on me daily," was his response. Brownsville was at least sixty miles from Raymondville and sixty miles from Pharr. He obviously planned with this thought in mind.

I was pleasantly surprised at how cozy the home felt. Of course, it needed a lot of decorating, or maybe a woman's touch to get it to my expectations, but I could work on that later. This was going to be our home, and I was thrilled! I was ready for nesting! Juan impressed Mamá incredibly by serving us baked beef roast with potatoes and carrots he had prepared for us so we could eat before our return trip back to Pharr. He even prepared a Jell-O for dessert! The men in our family would have never done that! He had been living in the home for the last six weeks, so he was comfortable now, even cooking occasionally.

Now the only formality left for the church was to publish the wedding band announcements, *las amonestaciones matrimoniales.* This requirement of the church is a public proclamation of the intention of the parties named to enter in the state of matrimony. This is a notice to anyone to make an objection if he/she knows of any reason why the marriage should not take place. The announcement, published for two Sundays prior to the wedding date, appeared in our meager half-page bulletin printed on both sides using cardstock paper.

A week before the wedding, Mamá asked me to sit down for a few minutes. She wanted to talk to me. She told me that after I get married, I was to do as Juan asked and that I was to obey him in all of his requests. I just listened. I suppose I already knew that because I always observed how Mamá always obeyed every command Papá gave her. I wondered, *Even if the request is unreasonable?* I did not ask why. I just sat there and wondered. I was very aware that the role of women in our family was to take care of men. I could cook, clean house, wash, iron, and even take care of my younger brothers and sisters, so I did not think that was an unusual piece of advice. I never really understood why Mamá felt she had to tell me that. I suppose it was her way of feeling that she had taken care of her duty as a mother to tell me what my role was to be as a wife.

Juan came over the Sunday before the wedding, and in front of me, Papá asked him to sit down on the couch. Papá began his lecture: "Aquí en esta familia nunca se ha metido ningún cabrón. Si, después de que te cases con Carmen te das cuenta que no es señorita, me la regresas a la casa. Quiero que la regreses si no es señorita." (No bastard has ever been allowed to come into this house. If, at any time after you marry Carmen you find out that she is not a senorita [virgin], bring her back to this family. I want her back.)

Juan was speechless, and I was in shock hearing those words coming out of his mouth. About the only thing he had not ordered me to do while growing up was to wear a chastity belt! Even with all of his rules in place, if I wanted to, I could have given up my virginity. Did Papá, as a parent, believe that it was his sole responsibility to make sure that his daughters remained virgins until marriage?

There were certainly opportunities presented to me many times during all those hours I spent out of the house at school. How was he to control where I spent every waking minute when he was at work or gone on his trips with the migrant workers? To remain a virgin was a personal decision I made by the time I entered high school. As I developed my relationship with Juan and countless hormones began to erupt as if they were life-forms invading my body like an uncontrollable case of the chicken pox, it certainly was not easy to keep my own personal commitment. Maybe if I were over thirty, I would have already succumbed to the hormones calling. I was only twenty-one years old! Why was Papá always so obsessed with virginity?

In his family, three of his four sisters married. Tía Julia, the eldest daughter, was the only sister who never married. Mamá told me once that Tía had a beau who lived in the neighborhood, but Papá Grande never allowed her to consider marriage. Why? Even if the expectation for the oldest daughter was to take care of her parents as they aged, I knew of many firstborn daughters who had married, and the husbands knew and accepted what was to be the inevitable responsibility for that daughter as the parents aged. Did something happen to Tía during the time when they migrated across the border to the United States, or during those tumultuous years when Pancho Villa was raiding the haciendas? All sorts of atrocities happened to women during that era. I knew it was the parents' responsibility to assure the daughters were taken care of, protected, and kept in a naïve state of mind until marriage. Sexuality was not a topic of discussion at any time in our family. I heard from Papa's regular lectures about setting my goals for life that all boys were supposed to stay away from me because they were all *cabrones* (bastards), and all they wanted was to take advantage of me. We, the daughters, were to remain as innocent as a child is of any carnal knowledge. In addition, Catholic teaching taught us that our bodies are sacred and merit respect at all times. Papá's never-ending endeavor to keep my sisters and me monitored at all times certainly reflected his lack of trust in our strength to withstand any carnal temptations. On the other hand, maybe he just did not trust any man, regardless of who he was or where he came from. Whatever led him to this thinking has remained a puzzle with me throughout my life.

The evening before the wedding, we had a rehearsal scheduled at the church. The rehearsal dinner was held at the Texan Hotel's Mandarin Room. Juan took care of the details for the dinner and arranged for Fr. Smith to join us for the meal. All the wedding parties were attended along with Fr. Haile and Fr. Barrett, our assistant pastor. Papá managed to behave himself and socialized with all members of the wedding party. All went well.

I woke up on my wedding day in a surreal state of mind. Is it really going to happen? Am I really going to the "Chapel of Love"? Everyone at home was calm. Papá and Mamá were quiet and seemed very reflective. I fixed the breakfast tortillas as usual. I had a morning appointment at the hairdresser, so I did not have time to fix lunch. I asked Lee to go out and buy a box of fried chicken for all of us so the kitchen would not have to be dirty. He complied. I often wondered who was going to help Mamá in the kitchen after I left. When I arrived home from the hairdresser, Mamá told me she was disappointed with the hairstyle I chose to wear. She wanted me to wear my hair loose and down to my shoulders. She had never expressed an opinion before, so I just picked a style that I wanted, all the hair pulled to the back with ringlets to the back. It was a perfect style for the veil I made.

We had a schedule for the use of the only bathroom in the house. All eleven of us, Papá, and Mamá had to shower and be ready for the wedding by 3:00 p.m. We were all to arrive at church thirty minutes before the 4:00 p.m. Mass. When Fr. Haile helped us plan for the wedding Mass time, he recommended that we have it at 4:00 p.m., and he would dispense us from having to attend Mass the following day, Sunday. Juan and I thought that was very thoughtful of him, so we agreed with that recommendation immediately.

Somehow, it all came together. Mamá helped me dress by helping me button all the back of my dress. All the family managed to get dressed and be ready by 3:30 p.m. Mamá made all my sisters' dresses to match the wedding-party dresses. They all looked great! My primeros padrinos arrived to pick me up almost an hour early. It was also a custom for the primeros padrinos to drive the bride to church and have the car decorated with fresh flowers, indicating the bride was in route to church. In addition, that car was to transport the bride and groom to the reception after Mass.

Before going to the church, Comadre and Fina came to see me in the wedding dress. They told Mamá they knew she was really going to miss all the help that I provided her with but that this is the destiny of all young girls . . . to start their own families.

At that moment, I realized why Mamá was so somber. I saw sadness in her eyes that I had never seen before. I suppose the reality of my leaving home was staring her in the face as Comadre and Fina reinforced what was imminent with their visit. My leaving home will definitely affect her household workload. It was now time for my sisters to step up to the plate.

I was still very nervous, wondering if Papá was going to decide the last minute not to show up at the church. Being very unpredictable with his reactive behaviors, he always managed to create stress for all the family. My brain was on overload just thinking of what it took me to get to this day. One more hurdle to handle at this time would truly break my tenacious spirit! Surely, I prayed, everything would go as planned! Taking a deep breath, I imagined my future with Juan would not have the constant stress that Papá always managed to create.

Mamá behind me, I walked to the living room where my padrinos were waiting with Papá. Madrina Panchita commented on how beautiful I looked. I just smiled and said *gracias*, as I knew that's what everyone says to all brides. Everyone was ready to go to church. I walked out of the house, realizing I had to stop next door to ask Tía Julia for a blessing, as was the custom for the family. Since Mama Grande had passed, Tía was now the elder of the Treviño family, and all nieces would go see her before going to church and ask for a blessing. Tía was waiting at her door and met me on the sidewalk and just hugged me and said, "Vaya con Dios, mi hijita" (Go with God, my child).

I proceeded to the car, sat in the backseat by myself, and my padrinos sat in the front seats. Papá and Mamá drove in their car with several of my sisters. The drive to the church did not even take five minutes. When we arrived, I must have been in a daze because I don't remember seeing anyone. I just knew that I was the last one to enter the church, and I stayed at the end of the line waiting for everyone to take his or her place. The church did not have a bride's room, so I had to wait at the entrance to the church along with everyone else. I just hoped that Juan managed to get all of his relatives to the wedding. I had not spoken to him all day!

Finally, everyone was in place; and the two priests, Fr. Donald Haile, OMI, and Fr. James Smith, OMI, emerge from the side entrance of the altar. The organist begins the processional Wagner's "Bridal Chorus" from *Lohengrin*, and the wedding party begins to process. Suddenly, I realized the church was full of people. When did they all get into the church?

Now it was time for me to process with Papá by my side. Papa's demeanor was as erect as a statue. He did not smile. I just held him by the elbow and processed with him, thanking God he did not change his mind about walking me down the aisle. We arrive at the altar. Papá is to hand me over to Juan. Where is Juan? The organist kept playing Wagner's wedding march. The bride arrived, but where is the groom? The priests are now turning their heads toward the side door, looking for the groom who is visibly nowhere. It seemed like hours! Did Juan decide not to show up? From the corner of my right eye, I saw a guest get out of a pew at the front of the church and headed toward the side door where Juan was to enter. The guest opened the door, and Juan and Beto, the best man, emerge as fast as they could. Someone forgot to unlock the door!

Juan shared with me later that all he could picture as he struggled to open the locked door was Papá standing inside the church, ready to pull the trigger of a two-barrel shotgun aimed directly at him.

Finally, we are all at the altar, and Papá hands me over to Juan. No kiss or hug! Both priests had a huge smile on their faces. The celebration of the Nuptial Mass began.

The exchange of vows takes place after the homily. During the homily, Fr. Haile shared with the guests that he was not very happy to perform this wedding ceremony because he was going to be losing his only organist and his Spanish tutor. Laughter erupts!

With the exception of the blessing of the *arras* and the *lazo*, the Nuptial Mass was celebrated in English. "Panis Angelicus" (Louis Lambillotte, SJ) was sung in Latin during the offertory, "O Lord, I Am Not Worthy" (Fr. Irvin, OFM Cap) during Communion, and Schubert's "Ave Maria" after Communion during my solo processional to present flowers to the statue of our Blessed Mother and to recite in silence the Memorare. The Memorare was always the first prayer I recited every time I stopped for a church visit on my return from college classes and passed by the church to go home. This prayer summons our Blessed Mother's intercession and protection and remains my favorite prayer of all prayers I learned during my Catholic school years:

Remember, O Most Gracious Virgin Mary, that never was it known that anyone who fled to Thy protection, implored Thy help or sought Thy intercession, was left unaided. Inspired by this confidence, I fly unto Thee, O Virgin of Virgins, my Mother; to Thee do I come, before thee I stand, sinful and sorrowful. O Mother of the Word Incarnate, despise not my petitions, but in Thy mercy, hear and answer me. Amen.

The custom of presenting flowers to our Blessed Mother always brought tears to the entire congregation. This last ritual reminded them that all the religious formalities have taken place, and now the bride is ready to take this leap of faith and begin her own family with her spouse. Will this groom be a good husband? Will he provide for her well-being? Will they be happy and have a lasting marriage? Will they be blessed with children? All of this inquires are left at Mary's altar in hopes that she will continue to intervene and provide the couple with aid in times of need. "Ya eres harina de otro costal!" (You now belong to a completely different sack of flour!)

Juan and I left the church, walking down the aisle to the playing of Mendelssohn's "Wedding March." We did it! Our grins were wider than any ocean on earth! Papa caught up with me at the outside of the church, hugged me, and kissed me. Actions speak louder than words! No words needed to be exchanged! Mama had tears in her eyes. Juan did not have to return me to Papá!

Let me tell you the secret that has led me to my goal. My strength lies solely in my tenacity. Louis Pasteur

Mama's hypertension did not improve with her age. Just like her father, she passed away of a massive stroke at the age of fifty-eight.

Papa lived to ripe old age. He passed away six day before his ninety-second birthday. On our twentieth wedding anniversary, he called me and shared with me that Juan was a good man and I made the right choice marrying him.

The Trevino Family with Bride and Groom; From Left to Right, Enrique, Imelda, Loreto, Carmen, Juan, Luis, Irene, Teresa; Front row from left to right, Esperanza, Maria, and Rosie.

Left, Papa and Mama, Carmen & Juan, Mama Sofia and Papa Gus.

From Left to right, Fr. James Smith, O. M. I. , Carmen, Juan and Fr. Donald Haile, O. M. I.

At the reception Juan displaying his contagious smile.

Mama's Favorite Homemade Birthday Cake

1234 Cake!

1 Cup Butter
2 Cups Sugar
3 Cups Flour
4 Eggs
1 Cup Milk
3 tsp Baking Powder
½ tsp Salt
1 tsp Vanilla
½ tsp Almond extract

Cream butter and sugar. Add eggs. Sift flour, baking powder, and salt. Add to creamed mixture alternately with milk. Fold in vanilla and almond extract. Pour in three 9" round baking pans. Bake at 350 degrees for 25 or 30 minutes.

Decorate with your favorite butter icing.

Pan De Polvo (original recipe from Mamá), a traditional cookie served at wedding receptions for good-luck wishes.

8 cups flour
2 cups sugar
1 cup lard
1 tsp cinnamon
1 egg
1 small can evaporated milk

Combine flour, sugar, and cinnamon in a bowl. Add lard and cut into flour mixture with two knives or pastry blender. Slowly add egg and milk; knead until smooth. Place on a lightly floured board and roll to 1/8-inch thickness. Cut into desired shapes. Place on cookie sheet and bake at 350-degree oven for 15 minutes. (Monitor after ten minutes to prevent excessive browning.) While cookies are warm, dust with a mixture of 1 cup sugar and 2 teaspoons cinnamon.

Pan De Polvo (later version)

Flour
2 cups Crisco shortening
1 cup sugar
1 egg
¼ teaspoon baking powder
4 tablespoons butter
½ cup milk
1 teaspoon vanilla
1 teaspoon cinnamon

Mix shortening with butter; add sugar and mix well. Add egg, baking powder, vanilla, milk, and cinnamon. Mix well. Add flour gradually until a smooth dough is formed. The consistency of the dough should be similar to that of biscuit dough. Roll out on a floured board to ¼" thick and cut into desired shapes. Bake at 350 degrees for 10-12 minutes. While cookies are warm, dust with a mixture of 1 cup sugar and 2 teaspoons cinnamon.

Makes about 200 cookies.

Buñuelos
Our family's New Year traditional cookie

3 cups sifted flour
1 teaspoon baking powder
1 teaspoon salt
2 tablespoons sugar
1/3 cup Crisco shortening
1¾ cup of anise-cinnamon tea
Vegetable oil for frying

Prepare tea by bringing to boil three cups of water, two tablespoons of anise seeds, and three sticks of cinnamon in a quart-size pot. Let stand until ready to use.

Have a one- to two-inch deep skillet half filled with oil ready to heat to 350 degrees.

In a large bowl, mix flour, baking powder, salt, and sugar. Work shortening into the flour with a pastry blender or with your hands. Gradually add the warm tea until a smooth dough forms. Knead until dough is smooth.

Form into balls. Roll out each ball very thin to 4-6 inches round in diameter circles. Fry in very hot skillet with oil until brown, about twenty to thirty seconds on each side. Drain on absorbent towels. Sprinkle with sugar-cinnamon mixture (1 cup sugar with 2 teaspoons of ground cinnamon) on both sides while warm. Store in airtight container. Makes about 36.

Tamales

½ lb. dried cornhusks (soaked in hot water to soften, then drained)
2 ½ lbs. boneless pork butt or shoulder roast
2 ½ quarts water
1 tsp dried oregano
1 tsp ground cumin
2 tbsp shortening or lard
1 cup chopped onions,
2 cloves garlic, minced
1 tsp salt
Chili Powder to taste

Masa Mixture

4 cups masa harina de maíz
⅔ cup lard or shortening
2 tsp salt
3 cups pork broth
⅓ cup lard or shortening, melted

Optional—add chili powder to add flavor and color to the masa, usually ¼ cup will enhance the flavor. Combine pork and water, simmer 40 to 50 minutes or until very tender. Drain, reserving broth. Break meat into shreds or use meat grinder to grind the meat into the consistency of hamburger meat. Transfer meat to skillet; add oregano, cumin, salt, garlic, and 1 cup of reserved pork broth. Mix well. Add additional broth if desired; stir until well mixed. Cook onions in 2 tbsp. shortening until tender. Add to meat mixture, mixing until blended. Stir in chili powder mixture to taste. Simmer 20 minutes.

In large bowl, combine Masa Harina with salt. Gradually begin adding broth to form a hard dough. Add the 2/3 cup shortening. Mix well and continue adding broth until the dough reaches a consistency of a thick pliable dough. Add the 1/3 cup melted shortening, mixing thoroughly. Dough is ready for spreading when it no longer sticks to your hand. To assemble the tamales, the cornhusks should have been soaking in hot water for at least an hour or more. Separate the husks and wash thoroughly. Stack to prepare for spreading. Take an amount of dough about the size of a golf ball, and spread the dough onto the husk, starting in the middle and working it outward to the edges of the husk. Leave at least two inches at the top of the husk that is pointed. The spreading can be done with either two thumbs or a large tablespoon. Fill the center of the husk with meat mixture. Fold the sides toward the center and fold the top end down toward the center folds. Repeat process until all dough is used.

To cook, use a pot tall enough to place tamales standing with the folded part resting down on the pot. Add enough water to cover ½ of the pot height. Cover, bring to a boil, and simmer for 20 minutes. Tamales are done when the husk is removed and the dough does not cling to it. Yields 3 dozen.

Coffee Cake
Our family baking project for the Christmas season.

Basic Sweet Dough
    ½ cup milk
    ½ cup butter or shortening
    ½ cup sugar
    2 eggs beaten at room temperature
    Additional melted butter
    1 teaspoon salt
    ½ cup warm water
    2 packages dry or compressed yeast
    4½ or 5 cups flour

Icing
    2 cups of confectioners' sugar
    2 tablespoons of milk
    1 teaspoon vanilla extract

Scald milk in small saucepan. Add butter or shortening, sugar, and salt.

Stir until dissolved. Cool to lukewarm.

Measure water into a large bowl. Sprinkle or crumble yeast over it and stir until dissolved. Stir in milk mixture and eggs; mix well. Stir in flour gradually. Mix until smooth. Turn out onto a lightly floured board. Knead until smooth and elastic. Place in a well-greased bowl (greased with shortening or butter). Brush top with melted butter and cover with dishtowel. Place in a warm place (my preference is on top of refrigerator) and allow to rise until double in size. Punch down, turn out again on a lightly floured board, and knead again for a few minutes. Roll out the dough into ¼-inch thick rectangle. Brush with melted butter, sprinkle sugar and cinnamon to taste, and add raisins (dried red and green cherries may be added for a festive look) as desired. Roll the dough tightly from one end toward the other end until it forms a roll. Pinch the ends together to seal.

Use kitchen scissors to slice about 3/4 into the roll. Width of slices may vary according to your preference. Place the cut roll onto a greased cookie sheet. It may be placed onto the cookie sheet forming a circle (resembling a wreath) or kept in a straight line. Additional melted butter and sugar and cinnamon mixture may be added on top. Bake at 350 F degrees for 25-30 minutes.

A white icing many be drizzled over the warm rolls if desired.

Summary

Journey to the Aisle . . . a Story of Cultural Expectations shares a life experience growing up in the barrio in South Texas where Spanish and Mexican cultural influences and traditions, being the norm, presented obstacles and conflicts while experiencing immersion into educational environments. Practicing Catholicism was the core of daily existence in the lives of families.

Growing up in a family with ten siblings, the author shares stories about learning how to survive daily in a male-dominant, Spanish-speaking home environment where gender roles were defined through unwritten rules. Attending an Irish Catholic school in the barrio and ultimately a public school system led to a journey of reflective questioning of cultural expectations.

She relates personal struggles and conflicts encountered as she journeys through the process of deciding to make a commitment to marrying.

Biography

Carmen Treviño Moreno, born to a Mexican immigrant father and an Italian American mother, received a BA degree from Pan American College in Edinburg, Texas, in 1965 and an MS degree in 1985 from the University of Houston at Clear Lake. After having four children and spending twelve years at home as a wife and mother, she returned to a career in education. After teaching home economics, English, and Spanish, she became an administrator in several districts in Texas. She is presently serving as chairman of the board of directors for Region IV Education Service Center, secretary of the United Way Bay Area Advisory Committee, and vice president of the Texas Association of Education Service Centers.